SHAPERS OF AMERICA

Barack Obama

The Politics of Hope

Shapers of America

Barack Obama
The Politics of Hope

WILLIAM MICHAEL DAVIS

Frontispiece: Barack Obama answers a question at a 2007 press conference.

OTTN Publishing
16 Risler Street
Stockton, NJ 08859
www.ottnpublishing.com

First printing

1 3 5 7 9 8 6 4 2

Library of Congress Cataloging-in-Publication Data

Davis, William, 1951-
  Barack Obama : the politics of hope / William Davis.
   ˙ p. cm. — (Shapers of America)
  Includes bibliographical references and index.
  ISBN-13: 978-1-59556-024-7 (hc)
  ISBN-10: 1-59556-024-6 (hc)
  ISBN-13: 978-1-59556-032-2 (pb)
  ISBN-10: 1-59556-032-7 (pb)
  1. Obama, Barack—Juvenile literature. 2. Legislators—United
States—Biography—Juvenile literature. 3. African American legisla-
tors—Biography—Juvenile literature. 4. United States. Congress.
Senate—Biography—Juvenile literature. 5. Presidential candidates—
United States—Biography—Juvenile literature. 6. Racially mixed
people—United States—Biography—Juvenile literature. I. Title.
  E901.1.O23D385 2008
  973.931092—dc22
  [B]
                                    2007024697

Table of Contents

Chapter 1

THE SPEECH

The FleetCenter, located in Boston, Massachusetts, has witnessed its share of dramatic moments. The arena is home to two professional sports franchises: the National Basketball Association's Boston Celtics and the National Hockey League's Boston Bruins. Some of the biggest names in rock and pop music have also entertained fans there.

In late July 2004, however, the FleetCenter hosted a different kind of spectacle. The Democratic Party had chosen Boston as the site of its national convention, and delegates from the 50 states, along with a horde of journalists, packed the arena for four days of speeches that would culminate in the nomination of Senator John Kerry for president of the United States.

Barack Obama delivers the keynote address at the 2004 Democratic National Convention. The speech—in which Obama placed his unusual personal history within the framework of the American dream—touched on themes of diversity, community, hope, and responsibility. It thrust the little-known Illinois state senator into the national spotlight.

"In No Other Country on Earth"

Shortly after nine o'clock on the evening of July 27, a tall, slim man bounded onto the stage at the FleetCenter. As he took his place at the podium, the assembled delegates erupted into thunderous applause. Many of them—like most Americans—knew little or nothing about this man,

Five days before his appearance at the Democratic National Convention, Obama pores over a draft of his keynote address. "The process by which I was selected as the keynote speaker," Obama would recall, "remains something of a mystery to me." He made the most of the opportunity, however, delivering a speech many observers ranked among the most riveting ever heard at a national convention.

who had been selected for one of the highest honors in American politics: the honor of addressing his party's convention as its keynote speaker.

He was an obscure state senator from Illinois with an unusual name: Barack Obama. He was a candidate for a vacant U.S. Senate seat but had yet to hold national office.

Obama waited for almost half a minute to let the applause subside. Then, in a rich baritone voice, he expressed his gratitude for the privilege of addressing the Democratic National Convention. "Tonight," he said, "is a particular honor for me because, let's face it, my presence on this stage is pretty unlikely."

His presence on the stage was indeed unlikely, and not just because he was a newcomer to national politics. Barack Obama, the son of a Kenyan father and a Kansan mother, had grown up in Hawaii and Indonesia. It was not a typical background for an American politician.

As Obama delivered his keynote address, he wove his unique personal story into a larger narrative about the promise of America. "I stand here," he said, "knowing that

A Skillful Writer

The keynote address to the 2004 Democratic National Convention—like most of the major speeches Barack Obama delivers—was written by Obama himself. This is somewhat unusual: most American politicians rely heavily on speechwriters.

Obama's writing skills are considerable, and he has two best-selling books to his credit. In the opinion of *Time* columnist Joe Klein, Obama's first book, *Dreams from My Father*, "may be the best-written memoir ever produced by an American politician."

my story is part of the larger American story, that I owe a debt to all of those who came before me, and that, in no other country on earth, is my story even possible."

He spoke a language of hope and optimism. He spoke a language of tolerance and dignity. And he spoke about common virtues and common dreams—the dreams of his white mother and grandparents, and the dreams of his black father and grandfather.

Obama acknowledged the power of individualism. But he also spoke of the connectedness of all Americans and the importance of community. "If there's a child on the south side of Chicago who can't read," he declared, "that matters to me, even if it's not my child. If there's a senior citizen somewhere who can't pay for her prescription and has to choose between medicine and the rent, that makes my life poorer, even if it's not my grandmother. If there's an Arab American family being rounded up without benefit of an attorney or due process, that threatens my civil liberties. It's that fundamental belief—I am my brother's keeper, I am my sister's keeper—that makes this country work. It's what allows us to pursue our individual dreams, yet still come together as a single American family."

He appealed to the better angels of a nation that had long been torn by acrimonious political fighting. To those who would continue to divide the nation for political gain, he declared that "there's not a liberal America and a conservative America—

Obama on Obama

I'm somebody who believes in this country and its institutions. But I often think they're broken.

there's the United States of America. There's not a black America and white America and Latino America and Asian America; there's the United States of America."

INTIMATIONS OF GREATNESS

Obama's speech held the convention delegates spellbound. Many observers judged the 17-minute oration among the most eloquent keynote addresses ever delivered.

Obama's personal appeal was also undeniable. His youthful good looks, his easy smile, and his charisma captivated viewers present at the convention and viewers who watched the keynote address on television. Some older convention-goers and news commentators were reminded of two much-loved politicians from an earlier time: John and Robert Kennedy. And some political observers openly wondered when Barack Obama would himself run for president.

Given that the 42-year-old Obama had yet to win election to the Senate, this was an extraordinary leap. But then, Barack Obama's life had already been an extraordinary and improbable odyssey.

Chapter 2 ROOTS OF A KENYAN KANSAN

Barack Hussein Obama was born in Honolulu, Hawaii, on August 4, 1961. His parents, who met while both were university students, could not have come from more different backgrounds. Barack's mother, Stanley Ann Dunham—her father had wanted a boy so much that he gave her his first name—was the daughter of two white Kansans who had lived in Kansas, Texas, Oklahoma, and Washington before settling in Honolulu. His father, Barack Obama Sr., came from a small village in rural Kenya. A brilliant student, he had won a scholarship to study at the University of Hawaii, becoming the first African student at the school.

Ann Dunham (she dropped her unusual first name before entering college) was 18 and Barack Obama 23 when they met in a Russian-language class at the university. They fell in love and decided to marry.

Initially, Ann's parents had reservations about their daughter's relationship with a black man. But eventually

With a father from Kenya, a mother from Kansas, and a childhood spent in Hawaii and Indonesia, Barack Obama has been dubbed a one-man melting pot. Here he is seen with his father's stepmother, Sarah Obama, whom he calls Granny.

Stan and Madelyn Dunham accepted Obama into the family. They were drawn by his intelligence, maturity, and friendly manner. He seemed a thoroughly likeable fellow.

Feelings toward a possible marriage between Ann Dunham and Barack Obama were decidedly different in Kenya. When his son wrote to announce his intention to wed an American, Hussein Onyango Obama strongly objected. Onyango, as he was called in Kenya, threatened to have his son's student visa revoked. He even wrote a letter to Stan Dunham, saying that he "didn't want the Obama blood sullied by a white woman." He opposed the union for other reasons as well. To begin, Barack Obama already had a wife and two children in his home village of Alego (also called Nyang'oma-Kogelo). While polygamy was still practiced in Kenya, Onyango doubted that an American woman would ever consent to sharing a husband. Nor was it likely that an American wife would agree to live in Kenya according to the traditions of the Obamas' tribe, the Luo—and Onyango wanted his son to return to the land of his birth.

A respected elder in his village, Onyango Hussein Obama was not a man to be trifled with. He had prospered as a farmer and knew the secrets of herbalism, curing diseases and helping heal wounds through the use of plant-derived medicines. Unlike many of his fellow Luo, he was not at all superstitious. Once, when a shaman (or what in the West is often called a medicine man) traveled to Alego to put a curse on one of Onyango's neighbors, Onyango beat the shaman and prevented him from entering the village.

Onyango was just as unyielding in his private life. He had been employed by the British colonial authorities in Kenya, and the experience seems to have led him to an appreciation of characteristically English virtues such as order and tidiness. He insisted that his family strictly observe these habits—to the point of driving one his wives back to her parents because she failed to satisfy his demands for things such as proper place settings at the dinner table.

Onyango's demands didn't stop with his insistence that family members observe European manners, however. He had great expectations for his son Barack, who displayed a supple mind from early childhood and whom he drove to excel academically. Although formal education beyond primary school was not at all commonplace for Kenyan natives in the British colony, Onyango desired that his son be "as educated as any white man." Onyango paid Barack's secondary-school fees. Although he was a brilliant student, Barack earned a reputation as a troublemaker, and he moved from school to school before winning a spot in the prestigious Maseno Mission School. After Barack was expelled from Maseno for disciplinary reasons, Onyango beat his son severely with a cane, then forbade him to live in the family compound until he had learned discipline.

A BRIEF MARRIAGE

Barack's scholarship to the University of Hawaii went far toward redeeming him in the eyes of his father. But the

A view of Honolulu, with the University of Hawaii campus in the foreground. Obama's parents met while both were students at the university.

rift between the two widened when Barack ignored Onyango's wishes and went ahead with his plans to marry Ann Dunham. He informed Onyango of the marriage only after the birth of his own son, Barack. The child's middle name, Hussein, was given in honor of his fraternal grandfather, but the gesture did little to placate Onyango.

If Barack Obama Sr.'s relations with his family in Kenya remained strained, his marriage was soon headed

The East African country of Kenya is the home of Barack Obama's paternal ancestors. His father grew up herding goats in the small village of Nyang'oma-Kogelo in southwestern Kenya.

for trouble as well. At the University of Hawaii he worked diligently, graduating in only three years—and at the top of his class—with a degree in econometrics (a field in which statistical methods are applied to the study of economic data). He had two scholarship offers to pursue a doctorate—one from the New School for Social Research in New York City and the other from Harvard University in Cambridge, Massachusetts. The former included a sizable stipend that would enable him to bring his wife and young son to New York. The latter covered only tuition, but in the end that is the offer he chose because he believed Harvard to be the more prestigious institution.

In 1963 the elder Barack Obama left Hawaii for Harvard, leaving behind his wife and two-year-old son. In the years that it took him to get his PhD, he never once returned to Hawaii to visit his family. The separation proved too much for Ann, who soon initiated divorce proceedings. The divorce was finalized in 1964.

Ann continued to work toward her degree at the University of Hawaii. She and young Barack, who had come to be called Barry, lived with her parents. To the toddler, Stan was "Gramps" and Madelyn "Toot"—short for "Tutu," which is Hawaiian for grandmother.

TALES OF AN ABSENT FATHER

Barry was a curious child, and his mother did her best to cultivate his inquisitive nature. Ann, who was studying anthropology, read him books about far-off places and different cultures.

In Barry's preschool years, the fact that his father was black and his mother and grandparents were white did not occur to him. And he certainly had no understanding of the significance of that fact. His father, whom Barry did not remember, existed for him only in a handful of old photos and in stories the family told frequently. In all these stories, Barack Obama was a towering figure—sometimes a bit domineering and inflexible but always a model of honesty, integrity, perseverance, and intellectual rigor.

In one story that Gramps especially liked to tell and Barry loved to hear, Barack and Ann were taking a friend, an African exchange student who had just arrived in Hawaii, on a sightseeing tour of Oahu. They stopped at Pali Lookout, where sheer cliffs drop more than 100 feet. As the three leaned on a railing and took in the panoramic view, Barack puffed on a pipe than Stan had given him for his birthday. He loved the pipe, smoking it nearly every night while he studied. When the friend asked for a puff, Barack passed the pipe to him. But as soon as he had taken a draw, the young man went into a coughing fit and dropped the pipe over the railing. Barack picked his friend up and helped him over the railing, demanding that he climb down the cliff and retrieve the pipe. The man was terrified. After a few minutes, Barack lifted the man back, settled him on his feet, and, giving him a couple pats on the back, suggested they go for a beer. Even after they had gotten home, Ann remained upset by the nerve-racking incident. Her husband could have dropped the man to his death. But Barack laughed off the whole matter, explaining, "I only wanted to teach the chap a lesson about the proper care of other people's property!"

In another story that Gramps told, he and several friends were at a local bar when Barack joined them after many hours of study. They were having a wonderful time, until a white man loudly complained to the bartender that he shouldn't have to drink "next to a nigger." A hush fell over the room and all eyes turned to Barack, who stood up. A fight seemed likely. However, Barack simply walked over to the man, smiled, and began to talk to him quietly about the foolishness of bigotry and the virtues of equality. "This fella felt so bad when Barack was finished that he reached into his pocket and gave Barack a hundred dollars on the spot," Gramps would note. "Paid for all our drinks . . . for the rest of the night—and your dad's rent for the rest of the month."

In his younger years, Barry did not comprehend the central role that race played in this story, but the moral strength and dignity of his absent father shone through clearly. "Your dad could handle just about any situation," Gramps observed, "and that made everybody like him."

TO INDONESIA

After her divorce, Barry's mother met and fell in love with an Indonesian exchange student named Lolo Soetoro, who was also studying at the University of Hawaii. By 1967 the couple had decided to marry. When his mother told him of these plans, six-year-old Barry knew enough to ask whether she really loved Lolo. Ann gave her son a reassuring hug.

Lolo returned to Indonesia while Ann arranged to join him there with Barry. In the months that it took Ann to obtain passports and visas, Lolo was drafted into the Indonesian army, which had been waging a brutal campaign against Communists and suspected dissenters. Hundreds of thousands of Indonesians were killed. Lolo survived a stint in the jungles of New Guinea and was assigned to work as an army geologist, surveying roads.

Although this job did not pay well, Lolo managed to build a small house in a village on the outskirts of Jakarta, the capital of Indonesia. When Ann and Barry arrived,

A view of Jakarta, Indonesia's capital. The Soetoro family lived on the outskirts of Jakarta and, later, inside the city between 1967 and 1971.

they found chickens, ducks, and a dog roaming the yard. These animals were joined by more exotic pets, including an ape named Tata, a cockatoo, and two birds of paradise. Two baby alligators lurked in a fenced-off pond.

To help with the family's expenses, Ann soon got a job in the U.S. embassy. There, she taught English to Indonesian businessmen.

Barry, meanwhile, ran the unpaved streets with the Indonesian children in what he recalled as "one long adventure, the bounty of a young boy's life." They chased chickens and captured crickets, rode water buffalo bareback, played soccer, and flew kites.

SCHOOL DAYS

Because Barry was six, it was time to begin school. His parents chose a recently opened Catholic school, Fransiskus Assisi, which was very close to their home and accepted children of all religious faiths. To enroll, students were required to register under one of five religions officially sanctioned by the Indonesian government: Catholicism, Protestantism, Islam, Buddhism, or Hinduism. Barry, documents show, was registered as a Muslim.

Yet there is scant evidence that the boy was actually raised as a Muslim—or as a follower of any other faith tradition, for that matter. His mother was never religious in the conventional sense. "She was interested in religions but didn't follow one. She was a freethinker," recalled Julia Suryakusuma, an Indonesian writer who was one of Ann Dunham's closest friends.

No. 203.

			L
1. Nama murid :		*Barry Soetoro*	P
2. Tempat dan tanggal lahir :	*Honolulu*	*4-8-61*	
3. Bangsa: a. Warga negara :	*Indonesia*		
b. Keturunan asing :			
c. Suku bangsa :			
4. Agama :	*Islam*		
5. Alamat murid :	*Ment. Dalam Roo1/Roo03*		
6. Dari sekolah mana (dipindahkan) dan kelas berapa :	*Taman Kanak Strada Asisi*		
7. a. Diterima disekolah ini tgl.:	*1-1-1968*		
b. Ditempatkan dikelas :	*1*		
8. a. Nama orang tua Aiah / Ibu	*L. Soetoro m.a.*		
b. Pekerdjaan :	*Peg. Dinas Geografi Dit. Top. A.D.*		
	(nama ibu diisi, hanja djika ajah sudah meninggal)		
c. Alamat :	*Ment. Dalam R1oo1/R003*		
9. a. Nama wali :			
	(hanja diisi, djika orang tua murid tak ada, sudah meninggal atau karena hal lain)		
b. Pekerdjaan :			
c. Alamat :			

Barry Soetoro's registration document for Fransiskus Assisi, a Catholic elementary school. On line 4, the first grader's religion was listed as Islam. That was the faith in which his stepfather had been raised, though friends and family members insist that Lolo Soetoro was not an observant Muslim.

"For my mother," Barack Obama noted in his 2006 book, *The Audacity of Hope*, "organized religion too often dressed up closed-mindedness in the garb of piety, cruelty and oppression in the cloak of righteousness."

For his part, Lolo Soetoro—like the overwhelming majority of Indonesians—was officially a Muslim. By all accounts, however, he was not very pious. Islam forbids the consumption of pork and alcohol, but Lolo ate bacon and "loved drinking" and other un-Islamic activities, according to his nephew Sonny Trisulo. Trisulo also said that his uncle was "the naughtiest one in the family."

Former teachers, friends, and acquaintances remember young Barry Soetoro, as he was then known, as polite, good-natured, and quiet. Early on, he struggled to learn the Indonesian language. He also stood out because of his black skin and his size: he was taller than his Indonesian classmates and—in contrast to the lanky Barack Obama of today—decidedly chubby. These differences made him the target of much teasing. "He was built like a bull," recalled Yunaldi Askiar, a former neighborhood friend. "So we'd get three kids together to fight him. But it was only playing."

One day, after an older boy stole his friend's soccer ball, Barry attempted to get it back and was hit on the side of the head with a rock. Seeing the welt, Lolo decided to teach his stepson how to defend himself. He showed Barry the classic stance of a boxer, and the two spent hours sparring in the yard. Lolo told Barry that a man must be strong—or, at the very least, have strong friends. Otherwise, he would be victimized by those who were strong.

Barry's first-grade teacher, Israella Pareira Darmawan, told a reporter in 2007 that her former student had tried to play the role of protector of the weak. "He would be very helpful with friends," she said. "He'd pick them up if they fell down. He would protect the smaller ones."

Barry had big dreams, recalled his third-grade teacher, Fermina Katarina Sinaga. When she assigned students to write about their goals for the future, Barry wrote that he wanted to be president. "He didn't say what country he wanted to be president of," Sinaga remembered. "But he wanted to make everybody happy."

Barack Obama's half sister Maya Soetoro-Ng, who was born in Indonesia in 1970, confirms that being chief executive was a notion her brother frequently entertained. "There was always a joke between my mom and Barack that he would be the first black president," Soetoro-Ng said in a 2007 interview.

Barry's mother had always been concerned about his education. "Five days a week," he recalled in his 1995

Barack Obama's half sister Maya Soetoro-Ng was born in Indonesia in 1970. She is seen here teaching a class at the University of Hawaii, where she is a professor in the Department of Educational Foundations.

memoir, *Dreams from My Father: A Story of Race and Inheritance*, "she came into my room at four in the morning, force-fed me breakfast, and proceeded to teach me my English lessons for three hours before I left for school and she left for work." During her son's third-grade year, she decided to remove him from the Catholic school and enroll him in a public school, State Elementary School Besuki. Now known as SDN Menteng No. 1, it was regarded as one of the best schools in Jakarta. It also had a predominantly Muslim student population, though it was not—as a conservative magazine and Fox News would later assert—a madrassa, or Muslim religious school. Nevertheless, two hours were set aside each week for religious instruction, according to administrators at Menteng No. 1, and

Barry Soetoro is circled in this detail from the 1969 third-grade class photo at State Elementary School Besuki. The public school was considered one of the best in Jakarta.

students registered as Muslims—as Barry was—studied Islam during these periods.

By this time, the Soetoro family's economic prospects had begun to look up. Mobil, an American oil company with operations in Indonesia, hired Lolo Soetoro as a government-relations manager. His higher salary enabled the family to move to one of Jakarta's nicest neighborhoods, which was favored by Indonesian businessmen and foreign diplomats.

Nevertheless, Barry's mother worried about the way life in Indonesia might be influencing her son's moral development. The Indonesian government was both repressive and corrupt, and Lolo accepted this as a given. In his view, one did whatever was necessary to survive and get ahead, including remaining silent about official abuses and cheating the system when possible.

"AMBUSH ATTACK"

In the face of this attitude, Barry's mother tried to instill in her son "the virtues of her midwestern past": values such as honesty, fairness, and perseverance. The fact that a person's life was hard, she said, was no justification for cutting corners. She held up Barry's absent father as an example. The elder Barack Obama had grown up poor, but he had achieved great success while still maintaining the highest principles—and Ann expected Barry to do the same. "Your brains, your character, you got from him," she told her son.

Black people in general also became examples of the high standards to which Barry should aspire. Ann brought home books about the American civil rights movement and copies of the speeches of Dr. Martin Luther King Jr. She told Barry stories of black children in the South who had only old and outdated textbooks passed down from

Accounts of the civil rights movement were a staple of the inspiring stories the young Barack Obama heard from his mother, particularly during the time they lived in Indonesia. This photo is from the March on Washington for Jobs and Freedom, August 28, 1963. During that event, Martin Luther King (seen at the center of the photo) delivered his famous "I Have a Dream" speech.

wealthier white schools, but who nonetheless became doctors, lawyers, and scientists. No burden was too great to be surmounted with integrity, hard work, and determination.

But Barry would absorb a different message one day when he was nine years old. The experience, he recalled in *Dreams from My Father*, was life altering; it caused him to begin questioning his race and all that the idea of race implies.

On that day, Barry accompanied his mother to the American embassy. She left him in the library while she went about her work. After finishing his homework, Barry searched for something to read and found a pile of *Life* magazines. As he leafed through the photo-filled newsmagazines, he played a game with himself. He examined each photograph and tried to guess what the accompanying story was about, only then reading the caption and article to verify whether his guess had been correct.

One photo showed a solitary figure—an elderly man dressed in a raincoat and wearing sunglasses—walking down a deserted road. Barry looked closely at the image, but he couldn't guess what the story might be about. What could be noteworthy about an old man walking along a road? Barry looked at the next page, which contained a close-up photo of the man's hands. The skin had an eerie, mottled quality that seemed almost ghostlike. Looking again at the first photograph, Barry noticed that all the man's features had the same uneven, ghoulish appearance. The man, Barry concluded, must be suffering from some terrible disease. But when he read the text, Barry discovered something altogether different: the man, who was black, had undergone a chemical treatment—and sustained irreversible damage to his skin—in order to lighten his complexion. He had wanted to pass as white. Thousands of other black Americans, the article explained, had paid for the same chemical treatments so that they could enjoy happiness as a white person.

In *Dreams from My Father*, Barack Obama depicted the incident at the embassy as a turning point in his life:

> I know that seeing that article was violent for me, an ambush attack. My mother had warned me about bigots—they were ignorant, uneducated people one should avoid. . . . I could correctly identify . . . cruelty in others, and sometimes even in myself. But that one photograph had told me something else: that there was a hidden enemy out there, one that could reach me without anyone's knowledge, not even my own. When I got home that night from the embassy library, I went into the bathroom and stood in front

of the mirror with all my senses and limbs seemingly intact, looking as I had always looked, and wondered if something was wrong with me. The alternative seemed no less frightening—that the adults around me lived in the midst of madness.

The initial flush of anxiety would pass, and I would spend my remaining year in Indonesia much as I had before. . . . But my vision had been permanently altered.

MEMORY AND MEMOIRS

In 2004, as Barack Obama was rising to national prominence, a *Chicago Sun-Times* columnist took a close look at *Dreams from My Father*. The columnist, Lynn Sweet, wrote that the book contained many made-up names and composite characters. This was hardly a revelation: Obama had admitted as much when the book was first published in 1995. "For the sake of compression," he wrote in the introduction to the first edition, "some of the characters that appear are composites of the people I've known. . . . With the exception of my family and a handful of public figures, the names of most characters have been changed for the sake of their privacy." Nevertheless, Sweet complained that average readers would have no way of separating the real people from the invented characters.

> ### Obama on Obama
>
> **"**What strikes me most when I think about the story of my family is a running strain of innocence, an innocence that seems unimaginable, even by the measure of childhood.**"**

28

Soon after Sweet's column appeared, other reporters sought to verify Obama's account of his life-altering day in the library of the U.S. embassy in Jakarta. According to archivists at *Life*, the magazine had never published an issue containing an article or photos about skin bleaching. When an interviewer brought this to Obama's attention, he responded, "It might have been an Ebony or it might have been . . . who knows what it was?" But archivists at *Ebony* magazine were also unable to find an article like the one Obama described in *Dreams from My Father*.

Conservative critics and political opponents seized on this and other discrepancies to call into question the basic truthfulness of the memoir—and, by implication, of Obama himself. They charged that he had distorted his life story for some personal or political agenda. However, the evidence they cited wasn't particularly compelling. The skin-bleaching episode, for example, would have occurred almost 25 years before Obama wrote *Dreams from My Father*. It is hardly surprising that his memory might be clouded by the passage of so much time. And beyond the details, the book has a degree of candor—including admissions of marijuana and cocaine use—that is difficult to reconcile with the suggestion that Obama deliberately misrepresented his past with an eye toward a future political career.

Perhaps most important, Obama never claimed to be presenting a journalistic account of his life—a fact critics often failed to note. On the contrary, as he said in the introduction, "what has found its way onto these pages is a record of a personal, interior journey—a boy's search for his father, and through that search a workable meaning for his life as a black American." And he readily acknowledged that incidents in the book did not always appear in strict chronological order; that much of the book relied on journals and oral histories of his family; and that the dialogue was "necessarily an approximation of what was actually said or relayed to me."

In any event, according to his account, questions of race and identity began to take on major significance for him in the wake of his experiences in Indonesia. The young Barry noticed that there weren't any people with dark skin—people who looked like him—in the Christmas catalog sent by his grandparents. And Santa himself was white. Sometimes the TV shows imported from the United States had black characters, yet they always seemed to play second fiddle to the whites. In America, apparently, it was preferable to be white rather than black.

Chapter 3 GROWING UP BLACK AND WHITE IN HAWAII

*I*n 1971 Barry's mother decided that it would be best if her son returned to Hawaii. The decision was most likely prompted by a couple of factors. Ann had concerns about the quality of the education Barry was getting in Indonesia. Beyond that, however, her marriage to Lolo Soetoro had disintegrated; the two would soon be divorced.

The plan was for 10-year-old Barry to proceed alone to Honolulu. Within a year, his mother and baby sister, Maya, would join him. In the meantime, Barry would attend school and live with his grandparents.

Ultimately, Stanley and Madelyn Dunham would do much more to raise Barry than simply looking after him for a year. In fact, he would live with Gramps and Toot, off and on, until leaving Hawaii for college.

KANSAS ROOTS

Stan Dunham, too, knew what it was like to grow up with an absent father: his had deserted the family when Stan was just a baby. His mother committed suicide when Stan was eight years old, after which the boy was raised by his grandparents in the small Kansas town of El Dorado.

Strong-willed and impulsive—some said wild—he was expelled from high school for punching the principal in the nose. The country was in the midst of the Great Depression, but he managed to support himself working on the oil rigs around Wichita and doing a variety of odd jobs on farms.

It was in Wichita that Stan met Madelyn Payne, who was four years his junior. She, too, lived in a small town in Kansas—Augusta—but her upbringing was much more conventional, as well as more privileged. Madelyn's parents were middle class and respectable, strict Methodists who shunned alcohol, gambling, and even dancing. They strongly disapproved of the boisterous Stan.

Nevertheless, Madelyn was drawn to the rowdy young man—who, when he wanted, "could charm the legs off the couch," according to acquaintances. In the spring of 1940, Madelyn's senior year of high school, she and Stan secretly married. She continued to live at her parents' house until graduation, only then informing her parents of her marriage.

Stan enlisted in the United States Army on December 8, 1941—one day after the Japanese bombed Pearl Harbor, drawing the United States into World War II. He would serve in Europe under General George Patton while Madelyn worked assembling B-29 bomber aircraft at the Boeing factory in Wichita. Stanley Ann, the Dunhams' daughter, was born in November 1942.

After the war, Stan enrolled in the University of California at Berkeley under the GI Bill. However, he quickly decided that college was not for him, dropped out, and moved his family back to El Dorado. There he managed a furniture store. But Stan was by nature restless and a dreamer, and the Dunhams moved frequently.

By 1960, however, they appeared to have settled down in Washington State. They'd been living in the Seattle area for five years and had bought a house on Mercer Island. Madelyn was working in a bank, and Stan had a steady job as a furniture salesman. Stanley Ann, a top student now in her senior year of high school, had gained early admission to the University of Chicago. But Stan learned of an opportunity he couldn't pass up: the furniture company for which he was working planned to open a store in Honolulu, and he jumped at the chance to go there. After Stanley Ann graduated, the Dunhams sold their house, packed up their belongings, and moved to Hawaii.

LIVING AMONG STRANGERS

Stan Dunham frequently clashed with his daughter, who was shy yet just as headstrong as her father. But by all accounts he adored his grandson, Barry. "Stanley loved that little boy," remembered Neil Abercrombie, who was a friend of the elder Barack Obama at the University of Hawaii and who is now a member of the U.S. House of Representatives. "In the absence of his father, there was not a kinder, more understanding man than Stanley Dunham. He was loving and generous."

However, by 1971 Barry had been living away from his grandparents for the better part of four years. Upon arriving in Hawaii from Indonesia, he would recall years later, "I realized that I was to live with strangers."

Barry thought his grandparents had changed quite a bit. They seemed to bicker continually. In the small, two-bedroom apartment they now rented in a Honolulu high-rise, it was impossible for Barry to escape their arguments.

Later he would recognize the source of much of the tension between his grandparents: Toot, who rose to the position of vice president of a local bank, was making more money than Gramps, who had left the furniture store to sell life insurance on commission.

If Gramps wasn't enjoying great financial success as an insurance salesman, his job did produce a big dividend for his grandson. Gramps's boss at the insurance agency was an alumnus of Punahou, a prestigious private school where Hawaii's wealthy elite sent their children. Although Punahou had a long waiting list, Gramps's boss had managed to get Barry in. It was his first experience with the oldest form of affirmative action.

In the fall of 1971, Barry entered Punahou School as a fifth grader. He would remember the transition as being somewhat difficult. Barry was one of only a couple new students in the fifth-grade class, and most of the children had been together since kindergarten. He also quickly became aware that his family circumstances did not much resemble those of his classmates. But most significantly, he was one of the few blacks in the entire school—a fact that, *Dreams from My Father* makes clear, led to much alienation and brooding throughout his years at Punahou.

While he did endure some teasing during his first months at Punahou, and while he revealed later that he felt like a misfit, teachers saw a well-adjusted child. "Barry was a happy kid," recalled Pal Eldredge, who taught math and science to fifth graders at Punahou. "He had a good sense of humor and was smiling all the time."

VISIT FROM A FATHER

In November 1971 Gramps and Toot received a surprising telegram. Barack Obama, Barry's long-lost father, was

Founded in 1841, Punahou—known as Oahu College between 1859 and 1934—is an elite private school. Obama attended Punahou from fifth grade through high school.

planning a one-month visit to Hawaii over the Christmas holidays. He had been in an automobile accident, and the doctors in Kenya thought it would be good for him to take some time off and travel.

Two weeks before the elder Obama's arrival, Barry's mother and sister Maya flew in from Indonesia. Ann busied herself preparing the downstairs apartment Gramps and Toot had sublet for her former husband. She also began telling Barry all about his father—who had remarried and now had five sons and a daughter in Africa—and about his homeland of Kenya. Barry read about his father's tribe, the Luo. He also read about Jomo Kenyatta, who helped lead Kenya to independence from Britain in 1963 and was elected the country's first prime minister.

Since 1964, Kenyatta had been serving as Kenya's president (an office he would hold until his death in 1978).

Barry arrived home from school one day and found his father waiting in the apartment, surrounded by his mother, Gramps, and Toot. Tall and straight-backed, he was dressed in a blue blazer and white shirt with a bright red ascot, looking every bit the English gentleman. After all the stories Barry had heard about his father, Barack Obama wasn't quite what he had expected. He was thin, perhaps even a bit frail, and he walked with a slight limp, the result of his car accident.

Barry's father gave him wood carvings of animals from Kenya. Although they didn't hold much appeal for a 10-year-old American boy, Barry politely thanked him for the gifts. At Christmas, his father gave Barry a more desirable present: a basketball.

Barry had awaited the visit with a vague sense of apprehension, but he grew accustomed to his father's presence. In the afternoons, the two of them would sometimes lie side by side on his father's bed, each engrossed in a book. One day his father put on a record of Kenyan music and taught Barry a traditional dance from Kenya. On several other days the whole family went sightseeing. During the evenings the adults would sit around talking about current events and telling stories about happy times in the past.

The visit seemed to be going well, but Barack Obama's imperious manner gradually got on the nerves of Gramps and Toot, and one night the tensions erupted into a bitter argument. Barry had turned on the television to watch *How the Grinch Stole Christmas*. His father told Barry to turn off the TV and go into his room to study so that the adults could talk. Toot told Barry that he could watch the program in his room, but her former son-in-law insisted that Barry study, saying that he spent too much time watching television and too little time on his schoolwork. Gramps and Toot were offended that an absentee father would give orders to a son they were raising, and in a house that wasn't his. Shouting and recriminations ensued.

After this unpleasant scene, Barry started counting the days until his father's departure. Before that, however, Barry would have to get through an event he was especially dreading. Mabel Hefty, his fifth-grade teacher at Punahou, had lived in Kenya for a time. When she heard about the elder Barack Obama's visit, she invited him to speak to her students. Unfortunately, Barry had told some of his classmates that his grandfather was "sort of like the king of the tribe," which made his father a prince. Furthermore, Barry said, he might become prince after his grandfather died and his father became king. After this story, classmates seemed

During his time at Punahou, Barry Obama left his mark in some wet cement outside the school cafeteria. The word "King," according to a school official, may have been written by someone else and is perhaps a reference to the fictitious story Obama told about his royal parentage.

to regard Barry with greater respect, but he was intensely afraid that his fibs would be exposed and he would be humiliated.

When Barry's father spoke before Punahou's fifth graders, however, his dignified bearing and commanding presence gave none of the children cause to doubt his regality. The elder Barack Obama told the children about the history, geography, and wildlife of his homeland. He discussed the customs of the Luo people. He talked about Kenya's struggle against British colonial rule, drawing parallels with the American Revolution, which had

This 1979 photograph is Barry Obama's high school senior portrait.

occurred two centuries earlier. He compared the way of life of Kenyans with that of Hawaiians. The children were captivated, and when he had finished they all applauded enthusiastically. Several classmates congratulated Barry for having such an interesting and important father.

The remainder of the visit raced by, and the day arrived for the elder Barack Obama to return to Kenya. Shortly afterward, Barry's mother and sister left for Indonesia. Ann and Maya would move back to Hawaii in 1973, but Barry never again saw his father.

"JUST A NORMAL KID"

As he progressed through Punahou's lower school and entered the high school, Punahou Academy, Barry seemed to have found his niche. He was a good student and a voracious reader with wide-ranging interests. Though he sometimes tended to be quiet, he had a circle of close friends. And he seemed at ease with everyone. "He was the kind of guy," remembered his friend Dan Hale, "who could walk into a room and navigate the cliques. My biggest impression of him was the way he could communicate with people. You always felt confident around him, no matter what group you belonged to."

Barry wrote for Punahou Academy's literary magazine and, during his freshman and sophomore years, sang in the school's choral group. But his real passion was basketball. Punahou was a basketball powerhouse, but Barry was good enough to make the varsity squad. He practiced constantly, teachers and schoolmates recall, dribbling a ball on his way to and from school, and shooting baskets at lunchtime. "He always had a basketball in his hands and was always looking for a pickup game," Larry Tavares, a former Punahou teammate, told an Associated Press reporter.

The 1979 staff of Ka Wai Ola, *Punahou Academy's literary magazine. Barry Obama contributed poetry to the publication.*

Punahou basketball players nicknamed their fiercely competitive teammate "Barry O'Bomber" for his accurate long-range jumper. On a Punahou team that won the Hawaii state championship in 1979, Barry wasn't a starter. But, according to former teammate Alan Lum, "He was a leader on the court. He would call people on it if they were doing something wrong."

To almost everyone who knew him as a teenager, Barry Obama appeared to be a cheerful, popular high school student. "He was just a normal kid," his homeroom teacher, Eric Kusunoki, remarked, "like everyone else."

Obama rises over a defender for a layup. During his senior year, the backup forward helped Punahou win the Hawaii state championship.

INNER TURMOIL

Yet he didn't feel like everyone else. He always felt like an outsider, he would reveal in *Dreams from My Father*. Despite the pleasant demeanor other people saw, he said, "I was engaged in a fitful interior struggle. I was trying to raise myself to be a black man in America, and beyond the given of my appearance, no one around me seemed to know exactly what that meant."

Classmates, teachers, and other people he encountered treated him differently because of his skin color, he says, and he seethed with anger and resentment. Sometimes the slights he suffered were unintentional, as when a white classmate assumed that because he was black he must enjoy the music of Stevie Wonder. Other times, however, they were born of a less disguised form of bigotry, as when an elderly white woman in his grandparents' apartment building rushed to the manager's office to report that a black man—Barry—had followed her into the elevator. The woman refused to apologize even after being informed that he lived in the building.

Yet whenever he started to resent white people in general, he couldn't help but think of his mother, Gramps, and Toot. They were white, but they weren't bigots. His feelings, Barack Obama would say in his memoir, were confusing and often difficult to sort out. "He struggled here with the idea that people were pushing an identity on him, what it meant to be a black man," his sister Maya later told the *New York Times*.

Interviewed years later, friends and teammates were surprised to learn of Barack Obama's racially based inner turmoil. "He never verbalized any of that," recalled Greg Orme, a former basketball teammate who regarded Barry Obama as one of his closest friends. "He was a very provocative thinker. He would bring up worldly topics far beyond his years. But we never talked race," Orme, who is white, told a reporter for the *Chicago Tribune*.

In his memoir, Barack Obama described his friendship with one of the few other black students at Punahou, whom he calls Ray. Ray, who was two years ahead of him, was like an older brother, helping him understand what it meant to be black in America. What it boiled down to, Ray believed, was that white people had the power. "It's their world, all right?" an angry Ray

Most teachers and classmates at Punahou remember Barry Obama as a cheerful, popular student. Yet, as he described in his 1995 memoir, Dreams from My Father, *he was "engaged in a fitful interior struggle," filled with racially based anger and angst.*

tells Barry in *Dreams from My Father*. "They own it, and we in it."

The real Ray, the *Wall Street Journal* reported and Barack Obama later confirmed, was Keith Kakugawa. Like Obama, Kakugawa is half black; he is also part Japanese and native Hawaiian. Kakugawa attested to his friend's inner turmoil. "He was going through a tough time. . . . I was probably the only one who didn't always see him smiling," Kakugawa told a *Wall Street Journal* reporter.

But, according to Kakugawa, Barry Obama's anguish had little to do with race. "It wasn't a race thing. Barry's biggest struggles then were missing his parents," Kakugawa insisted in a 2007 interview with the *Chicago Tribune*. "His biggest struggles were his feelings of abandonment."

Barry's father had always been absent. And, in 1976, his mother—having completed her coursework for a graduate degree in anthropology—decided to return to Indonesia to do her fieldwork. Barry, who would be entering his sophomore year in high school, begged to be allowed to stay in Hawaii. Gramps and Toot said he could live with them again, and his mother agreed. "I don't imagine the decision to let him stay behind was an easy one for anyone," Maya Soetoro-Ng, his sister, said. "But he wanted to remain at Punahou. He had friends there, he was comfortable there, and to a kid his age, that's all that mattered." Still, if Kakugawa's recollections are accurate, Barry resented the fact that "his mother was always pursuing her career."

"LIKE A FIST IN MY STOMACH"

From 1976 until his graduation from Punahou Academy in 1979, Barry lived with his grandparents. Their two-bedroom apartment was a hub of activity, a popular hangout for Barry's buddies. By all accounts, Barry's grandparents reveled in the constant comings and goings of Barry's friends, some of whom were close enough to the Dunhams to call them Gramps and Toot.

Race seemed not to be a concern in the household. Toot and Gramps welcomed all of Barry's companions. Gramps himself had numerous African American friends, mostly older men with whom he played bridge and poker.

But, Barack Obama would write in *Dreams from My Father,* an incident that occurred when he was in high school shook his image of his grandparents. One morning, Barry was awakened by an argument between Toot and Gramps. Toot, who always took the bus to the bank where she worked, wanted Gramps to drive her because the previous day she had been frightened at the bus stop by an aggressive panhandler. Gramps angrily refused. Barry said he could understand why his grandmother might be afraid of a man who blocked her path. Barry offered to drive Toot to work himself, saying it wasn't a big deal.

"It *is* a big deal," Gramps responded, shaking with fury. "It's a big deal to me. She's been bothered by men before. You know why she's so scared this time? I'll tell you why. Before you came in, she told me the fella was *black*. . . . And I just don't think that's right."

The revelation staggered Barry. "The words were like a fist in my stomach," he wrote in his memoir.

Eventually Gramps relented and drove Toot to work. Barry sat in the now-empty apartment and thought about his grandparents. "They had sacrificed again and again for me," he wrote in *Dreams from My Father*. "They had poured all their lingering hopes into my success. Never had they given me reason to doubt their love; I doubted if they ever would. And yet I knew that men who might easily have been my brothers could still inspire their rawest fears."

That night, Barry sought out one of his grandfather's African

Obama on Obama

I had to reconcile a lot of different threads growing up—race, class. For example, I was going to a fancy prep school, and my mother was on food stamps while she was getting her Ph.D.

American friends, an old poet he calls Frank in *Dreams from My Father*. When Barry related the details of what had happened in the morning, Frank offered him some troubling insights. Barry's grandfather, Frank said, was essentially a good person. Yet he could never know what it was like to be a black man, because he had not experienced the countless humiliations visited upon African Americans by white society. Toot, Frank said, had been right to be afraid of the panhandler at the bus stop. Unlike her husband, she understood "that black people have a reason to hate." Barry left Frank's house feeling, for the first time in his life, that he was completely alone.

In an effort to make sense of his experience, Barry devoured the books of famous African American authors, such as Langston Hughes, Richard Wright, Ralph Ellison, James Baldwin, and W. E. B. DuBois. But ultimately what he found in their words was anguish and self-doubt. The militant self-respect of Malcolm X resonated most with Barry. But, unlike the former Black Muslim, Barry had no desire to obliterate the white part of his identity—the bequest of his mother and Gramps and Toot. The color of his skin marked him, in the eyes of American

Obama, a voracious reader, consumed the works of such African American writers as (from top to bottom) Langston Hughes, W. E. B. DuBois, and Malcolm X.

society, as black. Yet, because he was also white, he felt pulled by two communities, belonging fully to neither.

In order to escape his anger, confusion, and anxiety, Barry turned to alcohol, marijuana, and, on occasion, cocaine during his junior and senior years of high school. His grades slipped. "Junkie. Pothead. That's where I'd been headed: the final, fatal role of the would-be black man," he wrote in *Dreams from My Father*.

However, in June 1979 Barry Obama graduated from Punahou Academy. He had plans to attend college on the mainland in the fall. In his senior yearbook entry he wrote, "We go play hoop." He also thanked his grandparents. But of his mother, who flew in from Indonesia for the graduation ceremony, he made no mention.

Chapter 4 COLLEGE YEARS

*I*n the fall of 1979, Barry Obama entered Occidental College, which had awarded him a full scholarship. Located in Los Angeles, the small, private liberal-arts college enjoyed a fine academic reputation. Oxy, as the school is popularly known, was founded in 1887.

Professors and fellow students at Oxy remember Obama for his keen intelligence, flair for writing, and self-assurance. Politics professor Roger Boesche called Obama "a very thoughtful student and a very curious student." Obama took Boesche's courses on American government and modern European political thought. Ken Sulzer, a classmate of Obama's in the latter course and now an attorney, marveled at Obama's ability "to sum [up] a whole lot of concepts and place them into a succinct written style."

Another classmate, Mark Dery, said, "I was impressed by the sharpness of Barry's intellect and, like many, his effortless charm." Dery now teaches journalism at New York University.

The student center at Occidental College. Obama attended Occidental, which is located in Los Angeles, on a full scholarship.

"Clearly the guy had a presence," Eric L. Newhall, a professor of English, noted. "He came off as a serious, articulate, intelligent young guy."

At Oxy, as at Punahou, Obama fed his passion for basketball. He regularly sought out pickup games. He also won a spot on Oxy's junior varsity team, which he helped lead to an undefeated season.

POLITICAL AWAKENING

Barack Obama recalls his years at Oxy as the time when his political consciousness awakened. In a 2004 interview with *Occidental*, the school's alumni magazine, he said, "I

got into politics at Occidental. I made a conscious decision to go into public policy." As Obama recounted in
Dreams from My Father, he also came to terms with his
racial identity while at Oxy.

The college's student body was more diverse than
Punahou's, and Obama hung out mainly with the other
minority students. He was, by his own admission, attempt-
ing to strike a pose as an authentic black man—a "conscious brother." During his freshman year, Obama recalled
in *Dreams from My Father*, he disparaged an African
American student named Tim as an Uncle Tom—a black
who is eager to win the approval of whites—because Tim
wore argyle sweaters, spoke like a wholesome white kid,
and planned to major in business. To Obama's surprise, his
friend Marcus—a conscious brother from St. Louis—gave
him a tongue-lashing in front of another black friend.

"Tim seems all right to me," Marcus told Obama. "He's
going about his business. Don't bother nobody. Seems to
me we should be worrying about whether our own stuff's
together instead of passing judgment on how other folks
are supposed to act."

The following year, Obama and several other Oxy students organized a campus rally to promote economic
divestment from South Africa. For decades South Africa's
white-dominated government had oppressed the country's
black majority through harsh security measures and a system of racial separation called apartheid. By the late
1970s, many human rights advocates were calling for the
international community to divest from (that is, end
investment in) South Africa as a way to pressure the government to change its policies toward blacks.

Obama and the other rally organizers at Oxy planned a
bit of street theater to dramatize the plight of South

Africa's repressed majority. Obama would speak briefly about the injustice of apartheid and the responsibility everyone had to end it. In the middle of his speech, two white students dressed as South African authorities would mount the stage and drag him off forcibly.

Obama, who had always been a gifted writer, worked diligently on his brief remarks. Witnesses say that his performance was mesmerizing.

"There's a struggle going on," he began. The crowd of several hundred didn't seem particularly receptive to a political demonstration. Some were playing Frisbee. Others chatted with their friends or lounged in the warm afternoon sun.

After pausing for dramatic effect, Obama continued. "It's happening an ocean away. But it's a struggle that

A rally to end apartheid in South Africa. It was at such a demonstration on the campus of Occidental College that Obama discovered his facility for inspiring people with his words.

51

touches each and every one of us. Whether we know it or not. Whether we want it or not. A struggle that demands we choose sides. Not between black and white. Not between rich and poor. No—it's a harder choice than that. It's a choice between dignity and servitude. Between fairness and injustice. Between commitment and indifference. A choice between right and wrong. . . ."

The crowd, which had fallen silent, erupted into clapping and cheering. Thrilled by his power to move people with his words, Obama grabbed the microphone to continue his oration. But just then, as planned, the students playing South African security officials seized him and dragged him off the stage to silence him. Obama recalled being genuinely disappointed, largely because he wanted to hear more applause.

RACIAL EPIPHANY

After the rally, the organizers got together for a party. The beer was flowing and the ashtrays were spilling over. Obama was in no mood to celebrate, however. He considered the rally, and his speech in particular, a farce. When a friend named Regina congratulated him on the speech, he told her that none of what they had done that day would have any effect—and the only reason he pretended otherwise was because it made him feel important.

Regina had no time for what she saw as his self-centered attitude. "You wanna know what your real problem is?" she asked. "You always think everything's about you. . . . The rally is about you. The speech is about you. The hurt is always your hurt."

In the midst of her lecture, a friend of Obama's named Reggie, who was drunk, wandered over and began talking about another party they'd had the previous year. They had trashed their dorm, Reggie said, laughing as he recounted how distressed the maids had been when they saw the mess they had to clean up.

Regina's grandmother had been a house cleaner, and she bristled at the insensitivity of the remark. "You think that's funny?" she asked Obama. "Is that what's real to you, Barack—making a mess for someone else to clean up?" Before he could respond, she stormed out of the room.

Later that night, brooding about Regina's recriminations, Obama had an epiphany. He thought about how he had earlier ridiculed Tim, and how his friend Marcus had told him to look at himself before passing judgment on someone else. He thought about what Regina had said: Stop thinking everything's about you. Stop counting on other people to clean up your mess. Obama realized that these were lessons his mother and his grandparents had tried to instill in him during his childhood, but at some point he'd tuned them out. Absorbed by his own grievances against "white authority," and fearful that unless he pretended to be something he wasn't, he would always remain an outsider—among blacks as well as whites—he had forgotten an essential truth. Values such as honesty, kindness, and responsibility aren't white or black. Character knows no color.

"My identity," Obama concluded in *Dreams from My Father*, "might begin with the fact of my race, but it didn't, couldn't, end there."

A New School, a Lost Opportunity

In the fall of 1981, after his sophomore year at Occidental, Obama transferred to Columbia University in New York City. He wanted to attend a larger school, Obama has said, and he also wanted to concentrate more on his studies. He was concerned that he did too much partying at Oxy.

A view of Columbia University's campus. Obama transferred to the Ivy League school, located in New York City, after his sophomore year. He received a BA in political science from Columbia in the spring of 1983.

Obama would write that he was a different person in New York. He stopped getting high. He ran to get fit and fasted on Sundays. He began calling himself Barack rather than Barry. During the summer of 1981, he says, he had brooded about his misspent youth and the condition of his soul. Now he was determined to make amends.

By all accounts, Obama applied himself seriously to his studies while at Columbia. Classmates recall that he spent long hours in the library but didn't seem to do very much socializing. As at Oxy, professors and fellow students alike were impressed by his intellect and his personal presence. "If I had to give one adjective to describe him, it is mature," remarked William Araiza, who had an international politics class with Obama at Columbia and is now an associate dean and professor at Loyola Law School in Los Angeles. "He was our age, but seemed older because of his poise and the calmness with which he conducted himself. . . . He had a kind of a breadth of perspective that a lot of us didn't have."

In the spring of 1983, Barack Obama graduated from Columbia with a BA in political science. Although his degree included a concentration in international affairs, his plans were to work domestically, and at the grassroots level. In New York he'd seen both racism and a casual acceptance of poverty alongside great wealth. He planned to work to change those blots on society.

One plan he'd long been tinkering with would never come to fruition. In 1982 Obama had received a phone call from his half sister in Kenya. She informed him that their father was dead. The Old Man, as his children in Africa called him, had been killed in an auto accident. Obama had wanted to travel to Kenya to visit the father he'd seen only once, when he was 10 years old. Unfortunately, he'd never found the time or the money, and now it was too late. Still, he recollected in *Dreams from My Father*, the news of his father's death didn't cause him pain, but "only a vague sense of an opportunity lost."

Chapter 5 COMMUNITY ORGANIZER

*D*uring his senior year at Columbia, Barack Obama had decided to become a community organizer. Essentially, community organizing is about empowering people to improve their lives by banding together to address their common problems. Individuals are easy for public officials to ignore; when many people are united in the pursuit of a common goal, however, officials tend to take their concerns more seriously—and to allocate them public resources. Community organizing emphasizes results over ideology. There are no litmus tests on specific issues. There is just the hard work of identifying a problem, convincing a group of people that it is in their self-interest to seek a solution together, and then figuring

---

Attending services at Chicago's Trinity United Church of Christ. Obama, who had been raised by an agnostic mother and non-churchgoing Protestant grandparents, joined Trinity's congregation during his years as a community organizer in Chicago.

out how to cajole or pressure politicians and government agencies into taking action.

Obama saw the need for fundamental change in American society, and he believed change would have to come from the bottom up. In his view, the administration of President Ronald Reagan—with the acquiescence of the U.S. Congress—had instituted policies that were devastating the most vulnerable Americans. He would help combat this trend; he would organize poor black people. And maybe hard-won progress in the black community would eventually spread outward, changing American society as a whole.

Obama's inspiration was the civil rights movement of the 1950s and 1960s. During that time blacks, led by figures such as Dr. Martin Luther King Jr. and joined by progressive Americans of all races, rallied around the cause of social justice. Through years of determined, principled action, they succeeded in changing the discriminatory laws and practices that had kept African Americans second-class citizens, particularly in the South. More important, they pricked the conscience of the nation, transforming many Americans' attitudes toward blacks.

If Obama hoped to find echoes of the civil rights era in community organizing, he was attracted to the work for another reason as well. He hoped to become, for the first time in his life, a part of the African American community.

In 1983 Obama wrote to every group and individual he thought might hire a community organizer: civil rights organizations, black elected officials, tenant advocacy groups, neighborhood councils. He got no replies.

He took a job as a research assistant at a Manhattan-based company that did consulting work for multinational corporations. After some months, he received a promotion to financial writer. The salary was good, but he continued to dream of working in the black community.

Obama quit his job with the consulting firm, after which he found a position in a Harlem-based organization that promoted recycling. But that job didn't satisfy his desire to effect grassroots change either.

OPPORTUNITY KNOCKS

Obama began to despair of ever finding a job in community organizing when he saw a help-wanted ad in the *New York Times*. The ad was for a Chicago-based group called the Calumet Community Religious Conference (CCRC), which sought a community organizer to work in Chicago's South Side. Obama eagerly responded. Soon he received a call from a man named Gerald Kellman, who arranged a meeting at a Manhattan coffeehouse.

Kellman, a native New Yorker, was a veteran community organizer who had worked on grassroots campaigns all over the country. His CCRC was trying to bring together residents of Chicago's predominantly white southern suburbs and the city's predominantly black South Side. These areas had been devastated by the decline of manufacturing, especially the steel industry, and Kellman's group was trying to secure jobs and municipal services to halt neighborhood decay. Kellman had set up a wing of the CCRC—called the Developing Communities Project, or DCP—

> **There's that side of [Obama] that's strongly idealistic, very much a dreamer. . . .**
>
> —Gerald Kellman, community organizer

to organize South Side residents. The only feasible approach, he believed, was to enlist the cooperation of the South Side's churches. Unfortunately, neither Kellman nor his two organizing partners, Mike Kruglik and Gregory Galluzzo, had been able to make any headway there. All three men were white, and the churches' black pastors eyed them with suspicion if not contempt. Kellman, therefore, needed an African American to head up the DCP.

After talking for a little while at the New York coffeehouse, Kellman offered Obama the DCP job on the spot. Obama accepted. The salary was meager—little more than $10,000—but Obama believed that an organizer's poverty attested to his integrity.

So in early 1985, Barack Obama bought a beat-up Honda with a couple thousand dollars Kellman had given him for moving expenses, loaded up his belongings, and drove the thousand miles from New York City to Chicago. He was 23 years old.

LESSONS FROM A MASTER AGITATOR

Community organizing, Gerald Kellman would observe, is "very romantic, until you do it." Obama dreamed of re-creating the heroics of the civil rights era, but he had little idea of what his new job would actually entail. Nor did he know much about Chicago. His education began right after his arrival in the Windy City.

The community organizers of the CCRC were followers of Saul Alinsky, a University of Chicago–trained criminologist who, in the late 1930s, established a neighborhood council in Chicago's notorious Back of the Yards district. The neighborhood council tamped down ethnic rivalries, reduced crime, and helped residents win concessions from the meatpacking businesses that were the major source of employment in the Back of the Yards.

From that point until his death in 1972, Alinsky worked on organizing campaigns in impoverished communities throughout the country, refined his rules for successful community organizing, and taught other organizers his methods. His ideas were controversial. Alinsky had no faith that elected officials would ever help the poor and the dispossessed because it was the right thing to do. Power alone, he believed, was what got things done, and power came from one of two sources: organized money (the tool of the establishment) and organized people (by which the

Community organizer Gerald Kellman, who hired Obama to work in Chicago's impoverished South Side. "Barack did not like direct confrontation. . . . He was more comfortable in dialogue with people," Kellman recalls. "But challenging power was not an issue for him."

poor could level the playing field). In Alinsky's view, the organizer's first task was to gain a clear understanding of power relations in the place in question. The second task was to mobilize the community. Again, this wasn't accomplished by appealing to people's sense of justice; it was accomplished by appealing to their self-interest. First, however, it was necessary to make them angry about their plight: Alinsky famously declared that the organizer should "rub raw the sores of discontent."

DIVIDED COMMUNITIES

From their small office in Chicago's Holy Rosary Church, at 113th Street and Calumet Avenue, Gerald Kellman and Mike Kruglik tutored their new community organizer in the ideas of Saul Alinsky. They sent him out into the

Saul Alinsky (1909–1972), the father of modern community organizing. Alinsky's tactics were highly confrontational. "Ridicule," he wrote, "is man's most potent weapon."

community to conduct one-on-one interviews in an effort to identify residents' self-interest, which would form the basis for organizing the community.

Kruglik told *New Republic* writer Ryan Lizza that, in his 10 years of training community organizers, Obama was the most gifted pupil he ever encountered. The young man from Hawaii had a talent for leading people to acknowledge the sources of dissatisfaction in their lives and then guiding them toward solutions. Kruglik remembered an incident that occurred shortly after Obama's arrival in Chicago, when the two of them were talking at a South Side coffee shop and a panhandler approached. Obama, Kruglik recalled, took the initiative, asking the beggar pointedly, "Now, young man, is that really what you want to be about? I mean, come on, don't you want to be better than that? Let's get yourself together."

Many acquaintances and fellow organizers have noted that, despite his youth and inexperience, Obama was remarkably self-assured from his first weeks in Chicago. "The guy was just totally comfortable with who he was and where he was," observed John Owens, Obama's assistant at the Developing Communities Project.

Despite his natural talents, Obama faced great obstacles in organizing Chicago's South Side communities. The distrust of pastors of the black churches—which were to serve as the linchpin of the DCP's organizing efforts—presented an unexpected challenge. Obama found mutual suspicions among pastors of different denominations. In addition, many South Side pastors had little in common with their suburban counterparts, and many resented the suburban churches' recruitment of their members. This made them resistant to the kind of city-suburban cooperation Kellman envisioned for his Calumet Community

Religious Conference. Perhaps most important, however, the South Side pastors were well aware that Obama's bosses were white men, and many of the pastors bristled at their attempts to organize the black community.

The distrust of the South Side pastors mirrored attitudes in the city as a whole. Chicago during the 1980s was torn by bitter racial divisions. In 1983, Harold Washington had been elected the city's first African American mayor.

Harold Washington, Chicago's first black mayor. Washington was revered by the city's African Americans, which complicated Barack Obama's community organizing efforts, as many people hesitated to express their complaints about city government for fear of undermining Washington's administration.

From the beginning of his term, a coalition of white alder-men led by the 10th Ward boss Ed Vrdolyak waged a no-holds-barred political war against Washington. Vrdolyak held the allegiance of a majority of aldermen, enabling him to stifle Washington's legislative agenda in city council, but he didn't control a large enough bloc to override the mayor's vetoes. In a city notorious for corruption, each side sought to steer patronage jobs, city contracts, and munici-pal services to its supporters while denying to its opponents the spoils of power.

Chicago's time-honored system of graft and patronage may have kept the core constituents of powerful politicians satisfied, but it ensured that many poor communities didn't get their fair share of public resources. Barack Obama was trying to organize underserved South Side communities such as Roseland and Riverdale. He found, however, that while many people were angry at conditions in their neighborhoods, they were reluctant to pressure city hall with their grievances. Many black Chicagoans consid-ered Harold Washington a hero, and they didn't want to give Ed Vrdolyak ammunition in his fight with the mayor.

THE PRAGMATIST

Obama, too, greatly admired Harold Washington, but he took a highly pragmatic view of Chicago's political battles. Loretta Augustine-Herron, a DCP member, recalled Obama's advice: "Whoever can help you reach your goal, that's who you work with. . . . There are no permanent friends, no permanent enemies." Following in the organiz-ing tradition of Saul Alinsky, Obama regarded results as what mattered most; ideology was unimportant.

Yet in some ways, Obama didn't follow the example of the father of community organizing. Alinsky's tactics were always highly confrontational and often outrageous. He delighted in publicly humiliating elected officials and civil servants. Obama favored a more restrained approach. He saw no need to embarrass people, particularly when they were only trying to protect their own job and when their ability to help members of the Developing Communities Project was limited. "Oftentimes," he told the *New Republic*'s Ryan Lizza, "these elected officials didn't have that much more power than the people they represented."

Obama, colleagues recall, excelled at what is called power analysis. He studied carefully the sources of power wielded by government officials or bureaucrats. And he understood that, in order to get something from these officials, communities had to approach them from a position of strength but still be willing to accommodate their needs. DCP members also say that Obama was a meticulous planner who insisted on educating the community and striving for broad consensus before taking action.

SMALL VICTORIES

Obama came to focus much of his organizing work on Altgeld Gardens. One of America's first public housing projects, the self-contained development in Chicago's far south Riverdale area was built in 1945. It was to be a model of urban planning. But over the decades it had become, in the words of Barack Obama, "a dump—and a place to house blacks." To the east of Altgeld lay the Lake Calumet landfill, the largest in the entire Midwest. To the south and west ran the Calumet River, so polluted that fish pulled out by the occasional angler were discolored and disfigured. To the north was a large sewage treatment plant. On many days the stench would seep through the windows and doors of Altgeld's nearly 2,000 run-down apartment units.

Apartment units of Chicago's Altgeld Gardens, the massive housing project where Obama focused much of his community organizing efforts.

Before Obama's arrival in Chicago, the Illinois state legislature had, with much fanfare, allocated half a million dollars for the establishment of a computerized job bank to help people put out of work by plant closures find new jobs. South Side residents had celebrated the establishment of the job bank—which was administered by the Mayor's Office of Education and Training (MET)—by holding a large rally. However, months passed with no one from the South Side's black neighborhoods being placed in a job.

One day, at a meeting in the MET office, Obama picked up a brochure touting the city's jobs program. He noticed that there were no MET outlets south of 95th Street, whereas 130th Street formed the northern boundary of Altgeld Gardens. Even though the projects were home to a city's worth of unemployed, there were no official job-placement resources within 35 blocks. Obama had an issue upon which to move. He believed Altgeld residents would see that bringing MET resources south was clearly in their self-interest.

He was right. Obama and his Developing Communities Project mobilized Altgeld residents, petitioning city officials and holding rallies in support of bringing the jobs program into their neighborhood. Eventually, Mayor Washington agreed to their request. Gaining access to the job bank didn't solve Altgeld's unemployment problem. Still, it was a tangible victory.

Although frustrations and defeats still greatly outnumbered the small victories, Obama had begun to see his work pay some dividends after a year in Chicago. The DCP organized neighborhood cleanups, sponsored career days for area youth, and won agreements from aldermen to improve sanitation services and overhaul run-down parks. Streets were being repaired, sewers cleaned out, and crime watch programs instituted.

Then, in 1986, the DCP's highest-profile issue arose. A legal notice in the classified section of a local newspaper announced that the Chicago Housing Authority (CHA), which ran Altgeld Gardens, was taking bids to remove asbestos from its on-site management office. Asbestos, an insulating material that was widely used on pipes in older construction, causes lung cancer if fibers become airborne and are inhaled. Seeing the legal notice, someone (Obama credits a DCP member, while Gerald Kellman insists it was Obama himself) wondered: If asbestos is in the CHA office, isn't it likely to be in residents' apartments as well? After all, they were constructed at the same time.

Obama urged the residents of Altgeld to request that their apartments be tested for asbestos and, if any were found on the pipes, that it be removed. But these requests were ignored by the CHA bureaucracy.

The residents persevered. Obama helped organize a bus trip, and he and a handful of Altgeld residents went to the downtown Chicago office of the CHA to meet with the agency's director. Initially, they were told that the director was unavailable and that they should leave. But the residents had issued a press release announcing their visit, and when news crews began arriving at the office, the CHA director's assistant hastily scheduled a meeting later at Altgeld.

On the evening of that meeting, hundreds of Altgeld residents packed a school gymnasium. Print reporters and TV news crews were on hand to cover the event. Unfortunately, the meeting quickly degenerated into a chaotic shouting match, and the CHA director beat a hasty retreat before addressing residents' concerns.

Nevertheless, the publicity ultimately appears to have pressured the CHA into taking action. The Altgeld Gardens apartments were tested and found to have asbestos, which was eventually removed. Yet even this, as Obama noted in his memoir, was only a partial victory: the costs of taking care of the asbestos problem meant that other needed work on Altgeld units, including upgraded plumbing, could not be done.

This is the way it was in community organizing. The victories were modest, the frustrations seemingly endless.

Still, Obama pressed on. Working with a local teacher and school principal, he helped spearhead a program to provide teens with tutoring and mentorship. He championed efforts to get parents involved in school reform. He organized South Side and Southeast Side communities to address environmental issues.

FINDING A SPIRITUAL HOME

Obama continued to enlist black church leaders, with varying degrees of success, in the DCP's community-building efforts. One day a pastor asked him a pointed question: Why don't *you* go to church? Perhaps, the pastor suggested, church leaders might be more apt to work with Obama if they saw that he shared their religious commitment.

Obama thought about this. He had not been raised in any particular faith. His mother approached religion from an anthropological perspective; she was interested in the religious practices of various cultures but was herself a nonbeliever. By the time he lived with his grandparents, Toot and Gramps—who had both grown up as Protestants—had ceased attending services. Although Obama had been exposed to Catholicism and Islam as a boy in Indonesia, neither had made much of an impression on him.

Obama recognized the important role that the black church had played in sustaining African Americans through the trials of slavery, the Jim Crow era of segregation in the South, and the struggle for civil rights. In addition to offering uplift to the spirit, the church had been at the center of black political, economic, and social life. And now, Obama recalled years later, he longed to be part of a spiritual community.

Several of the ministers he met had mentioned a dynamic preacher named Reverend Jeremiah Wright Jr., pastor of Chicago's Trinity United Church of Christ. Since 1972, when he took over as pastor of Trinity, Wright had grown his congregation from only 200 to nearly 4,000 members. Wright's church attracted large numbers of young black

Jeremiah Wright Jr. preaches to his congregation at the Trinity United Church of Christ. Wright's emphasis on African heritage and the African American experience was a large part of what attracted Obama to Trinity.

professionals, such as doctors, lawyers, academics, and business leaders. This was probably due to the emphasis the pastor—a holder of master's and doctoral degrees—placed on scholarship. Wright's church also stressed the common African heritage and African American experience of its members: its motto was "Unashamedly Black and Unapologetically Christian," and its stated goals included "a congregation with a non-negotiable commitment to Africa" and "a congregation committed to the historical education of African people in diaspora."

Barack Obama acknowledged that "there was an explicitly political aspect to the mission and message of Trinity at that time that I found appealing." But he also conceded that part of his attraction to Trinity was that it had no affiliation with the Developing Communities Project. "If I joined one of the churches I was already organizing," Obama said, "that might have caused some tensions." In any event, he became a member of Trinity's congregation, and over the years Jeremiah Wright would become a close confidant and trusted spiritual adviser.

LESSONS FROM A FATHER'S FAILURES

While Barack Obama was in Chicago working as a community organizer, his half sister Auma paid him a visit. Auma Obama was the daughter of the senior Barack Obama and his first wife. She had grown up in Kenya. During her visit to Chicago, she told her brother endless stories of life in that country, and of his extended family there.

She also told him about his father. She said that, after returning to Kenya with a degree from Harvard University, the Old Man had prospered. At first he had worked for an American oil company, making a great deal of money. Then he took a prestigious position as an economist with Kenya's Ministry of Tourism. He appeared to be on his way to a successful career in government. However, in the mid-1960s tensions between Kenya's two largest tribes, the Kikuyus and the Luos, began to surface. The president of Kenya, Jomo Kenyatta, was a Kikuyu, and Luos grumbled about all the corruption that benefited his fellow tribesmen. The Old Man, Auma said, complained vociferously that unqualified people were getting all the top government posts. He believed that, with his intelligence, education, and experience, he deserved to be promoted. But he was a Luo. Eventually government leaders had him fired from his job at the Ministry of Tourism, prohibited him from working in any other government post, and warned foreign companies wishing to do business in Kenya not to hire him. Finally, he got a rather insignificant post with the Kenyan Water Department. It was little more than a bookkeeping job, and he had a PhD in economics.

Embittered, he took to drinking heavily and, Auma said, may have been drunk when he got into the car accident from which he was recovering when he visited Hawaii in 1971. That accident had kept him out of work for a year, and when he was finally ready to return to his job at the Water Department, he found out that he had been fired. He had no money but tried to maintain the illusion that he was still an important man. He borrowed from friends and acquaintances, promising to repay his debts when he was back on his feet, yet eventually no one would lend him any more money. He continued to drink excessively and, it was believed, was driving drunk when he crashed his car and killed himself in 1982.

Sarah Obama holds a photograph of her stepson at his gravesite in the Kenyan village of Nyang'oma-Kogelo. Barack Obama's father died, bitter and disillusioned, in 1982.

Barack Obama was stunned to hear about the circumstances surrounding his father's death. The great tribal prince of his imagination had died a frail, lonely, defeated man.

In 1987, after Auma's visit, Obama and Gerald Kellman traveled to Harvard University to attend a conference. Obama, Kellman recalls, spoke about how his father's spirit had been crushed because he had not been able to fulfill his dreams and ambitions. "He talked about what happens to you," Kellman told a reporter, "if you're not practical in finding ways to do things effectively." Perhaps, Obama confessed to his mentor, he might better be able to pursue his goal of changing society by going to law school and entering politics.

Chapter 6 HARVARD LAW

Harvard Law School—located in Cambridge, Massachusetts, just across the Charles River from Boston—is arguably the best law school in America. Each year more than 7,000 high-achieving college graduates from all over the United States and from about 100 foreign countries apply for admission. The approximately 500 who are accepted gain a unique opportunity: to study under some of America's most brilliant and distinguished legal minds.

Barack Obama entered Harvard Law School during the fall semester of 1988. At 27, he was several years older than most of his classmates. Ahead lay three years of hard work and intellectual challenges. He would have to learn the law of contracts; the law of property (both personal and real estate); criminal law, civil law, and their procedure in court. He would have to master the art of legal research. He would have to learn to write briefs and prepare cases. There were other courses he would have to take, involving new and specialized kinds of law, as well as specific issues in the law. And there was constitutional law—the study of the U.S. Constitution and how it has been interpreted in American history both to keep people in bondage and to set people free. This was the area of the law that interested Obama the most.

EXPLORING AFRICA

In February of 1988, Obama had received his acceptance letter from Harvard Law School. He informed his colleagues at the Developing Communities Project that he would be leaving but remained on the job until May.

Over the summer he finally did something he'd been meaning to do for years: he visited Kenya, the homeland of his father. In the company of Auma, he spent several

Malik Obama holds a photograph of himself, his famous half brother, and a friend. The photo was taken during Barack Obama's 1988 trip to Kenya.

weeks meeting a seemingly endless line of relatives—aunts, uncles, cousins, a grandmother. All greeted their American kinsman warmly.

Obama's relatives shared stories about his father and his grandfather. Just as his image of his father had changed dramatically with the stories Auma had told him, now he found his image of Hussein Onyango Obama, his grandfather, altered by new information. He learned that Onyango—the great tribal elder, leader of his village—had been ostracized by his family and by the village of his birth because he had adopted the ways of the British. Onyango, it turned out, had served the British as a domestic servant, a cook. The fierce, independent grandfather of Obama's imagination now seemed, he would say, a bit like an Uncle Tom.

Barack Obama would write movingly of his trip to Kenya in the final section of *Dreams from My Father*. He would describe how, when he met his stepgrandmother in the small village where his father grew up, the old woman told him that he had finally come home. On the wall of her small house, he would relate, hung her stepson's diploma from Harvard. And Obama would tell of visiting the gravesites of his father and grandfather, which were under a mango tree, at the edge of a cornfield. A simple plaque on his grandfather's grave bore Hussein Onyango Obama's name and the dates of his birth and death. His father's grave, after six years, remained unmarked.

Both men had been proud and ambitious, and both had died lost and lonely. Life, Obama realized, had defeated both men's spirits—his father's because he had lacked "a faith born out of hardship, a faith that wasn't new, that wasn't black or white or Christian or Muslim but that pulsed in the heart of the first African village and the first Kansas homestead—a faith in other people."

LAW STUDENT

After returning from his trip to Kenya, Barack Obama tied up loose ends in Chicago, where he'd lived for more than three years. He said goodbye to friends and former organizing colleagues. He got rid of his old Honda, which was failing, and bought another used car for $500. After packing his meager possessions into the car, he made the long drive east to Cambridge.

At Harvard, Obama threw himself into his studies. He rented a basement apartment north of Cambridge, in Somerville. And, classmates recall, he generally avoided parties.

Professors and fellow students quickly recognized his extraordinary intellectual gifts as well as his interpersonal skills. Harvard law professor David B. Wilkins remembered Obama as "brilliant, charismatic, and focused." Crystal Nix Hines, a former classmate, was struck by Obama's respect for other people's points of view. "A lot of people at the time were just talking past each other," Nix Hines, who is now a television writer, told the *Boston Globe*, "very committed to their opinions, their point of view, and not particularly interested in what other people had to say. Barack transcended that."

By the end of his first year, Obama ranked near the top of his class. His high grades, along with his entry in a writing competition, qualified him for a slot on the *Harvard Law Review*. Only the top students from the second- and third-year classes may serve as editors of Harvard's prestigious law journal, which publishes articles by professors, legal scholars, and other leading professionals.

During the late 1980s and early 1990s, the *Law Review* was a political tinderbox, with conservative and liberal editors battling each other bitterly and incessantly. "I have worked in the Supreme Court and the White House," recalled Bradford Berenson, a contemporary of Obama's, in 2007, "and I never saw politics as bitter as at Harvard Law Review." The stakes were high: *Harvard Law Review* is America's premier legal journal, and the inclusion or exclusion of a certain paper could advance or set back a particular political agenda.

The divisions among the *Law Review* staff were mirrored in the law school as a whole, which Berenson said "was populated by a bunch of would-be Daniel Websters harnessed to extreme political ideologies." Racial and gender politics added to the incendiary mix. Minority students and liberals demanded more diversity on the faculty; conservatives decried any hint of affirmative action.

The 1989–1990 academic year was marked by especially heated passions at Harvard. During the fall semester, as Obama entered his second year in law school, liberal and minority students began staging demonstrations and sit-ins to protest the lack of diversity on the law school faculty. During the spring semester Derrick Bell, Harvard Law School's first tenured African American professor, quit the school because of the administration's failure to grant tenure to an African American woman.

Obama was a member of the Black Law Students Association, which was at the forefront of the demands for diversity. Yet, former classmates and professors recall, he was not as strident as many BLSA members and other protesters. His instinct was to seek common ground rather than to stoke further confrontation. "Barack was a stabilizing influence in that he would absolutely support [the diversity] efforts," noted Harvard law professor Charles J. Ogletree Jr., who is also African American, "but

[he] was also someone who could discuss and debate them with students or faculty who had different views."

TRAILBLAZER

By his second year, classmates were urging Obama to run for president of the *Harvard Law Review*. He initially declined because, as he told friends, the position would simply be a detour in his long-range plan to resume community-organizing activities in Chicago. In fact, Obama would confess that he sometimes questioned why he was even attending law school. "I worried that it represented the abandonment of my youthful ideals, a concession to the hard realities of money and power," he revealed in *The Audacity of Hope*.

Eventually, however, Obama changed his mind about seeking the presidency of the *Harvard Law Review*. According to Kenneth Mack, an African American classmate of Obama's who currently teaches at Harvard Law School, Obama made that decision at the urging of an older black student. The student had thought it important for African Americans to compete for the *Law Review*'s top post, which no black had ever held. But Obama also told some of his friends that he might be able to dampen the hostility between the journal's conservative and liberal factions.

Election of the *Law Review* president was a grueling, daylong process. It took place on February 5, 1990. Nineteen candidates were vying for the position, and the remaining 61 editors verbally dissected each one. Every couple hours, the editors dismissed several candidates whom they found wanting. After all the conservatives had been eliminated and the field had been winnowed to a few candidates, conservative editors threw their support behind Obama. "Whatever his politics," Bradford Berenson recalled, "we felt he would give us a fair shake."

Barack Obama thus became the first black president in the 100-year history of the *Harvard Law Review*. The milestone drew a brief flurry of media attention. Reporters descended on Cambridge to interview Obama. Actor Blair Underwood, who played a young African American lawyer on the TV series *L.A. Law*, talked to Obama to gather material for his character. A publisher commissioned Obama to write a book about how he had arrived at this point in his life. Five years later, he would complete *Dreams from My Father*.

In the meantime, Obama had to manage the *Harvard Law Review*, to say nothing of completing the coursework

Members of the Harvard Law Review *staff, 1990. Barack Obama, the first black president in the* Law Review's *100-year history, is at the center of the photo.*

for his law degree. His *Law Review* responsibilities alone—
which included evaluating dozens of articles submitted for
publication and presiding over editorial meetings—
required some 50 to 60 hours each week.

Staff members who had hoped he could end the parti-
san fighting on the journal were not disappointed. All who
were interviewed in 2007 for a *New York Times* article
remembered Obama as a consensus-builder, fair-minded
and a good listener. "He was in part effective because he
didn't make things about his personal sentiment," recalled
Nancy McCullough, who is now an entertainment lawyer.
"He made it about the group sentiment and what the
group majority might agree to."

Indeed, discerning just what Obama's personal sentiment was on a particular issue could be difficult, according

*Kenneth Mack, now a law
professor at Harvard, was
Obama's classmate and
also served as an editor of
the* Law Review. *Obama,
Mack recalls, "was
grounded, comfortable in
his own skin, knew who he
was, where he came from,
why he believed things."*

to several former classmates, *Law Review* editors, and professors. This was due not only to his tendency to avoid bitter ideological arguments but also to his willingness and ability to evaluate multiple sides of an issue. "He then and now is very hard to pin down," observes Kenneth Mack, who served as an editor under Obama. Professor Charles Ogletree Jr. expressed this in different terms. "He can enter your space and organize your thoughts," Ogletree told the *New York Times*, "without necessarily revealing his own concerns and conflicts."

The life story of Harvard's most celebrated minority student appeared to validate the views of campus conservatives and liberals alike. Obama's brilliance was undeniable, and conservatives could say that he had succeeded at Harvard exclusively on his own merit. On the other hand, Obama thought that he previously had benefited from affirmative action, which liberals could cite as confirmation of their belief in the appropriateness of leveling the playing field for members of disadvantaged groups.

Obama's political skills and leadership were confirmed by events at the *Harvard Law Review* after his term as president had expired. Under his successor, the nasty

> " **[Obama is] one of the two most talented students I've had in 37 years in teaching. . . . When I look at my kids and grandkids and ask what makes me hopeful about the future—one thing is Barack Obama.** "
>
> —Laurence Tribe, Harvard Law School professor and constitutional scholar

ideological partisanship that he had managed to tame erupted anew. "The years that followed [Obama's tenure] at the law review," recalled former editor Julius Genachowski, "were very difficult. I think what that says is, the place was a powder keg that had the potential to go off, and it's relevant that it didn't explode during his tenure."

A CLARION CALL

In the spring of his senior year, Barack Obama received a high honor from the Black Law Students Association. The BLSA traditionally invited a distinguished judge or professor to deliver the keynote address at its annual conference. But Obama was tapped to give the 1991 address. By all accounts, he delivered an eloquent and moving appeal for social responsibility. "It was a clarion call," Harvard law professor Randall L. Kennedy recalled. "We've gotten this education, we've gotten this great halo, this great career-enhancing benefit. Let's not just feather our nests. Let's go forward and address the many ills that confront our society."

In 1991 Obama was awarded a JD (doctor of laws) degree from Harvard. He graduated magna cum laude.

Chapter

7 PUTTING DOWN ROOTS

*H*aving graduated with high honors from one of the nation's premier law schools—especially after serving as president of the *Harvard Law Review*—Barack Obama had career opportunities that were virtually unlimited. Actually, recruiters began contacting him with job offers well before he had officially received his law degree. One attorney who called the *Harvard Law Review* in early 1991 in an effort to recruit Obama to his firm was told by a secretary, "You can leave your name and take a number. You're No. 647."

Obama could easily have burnished his legal credentials with a prestigious clerkship. Abner Mikva, Chief Judge of the United States Court of Appeals for the D.C. Circuit, attempted to recruit Obama as a clerk. That position, legal experts say, would have opened the way for Obama to clerk for a Supreme Court justice. However, Obama declined Mikva's offer.

Obama, who turned 30 in August 1991, could have opted for a high salary and put himself on a path to a lifetime of wealth, comfort, and status. Recruiters from the nation's top law firms dangled lucrative offers. "He could have gone to the most opulent of law firms," said David Axelrod, who currently serves as Obama's media adviser. "After Harvard, Obama could have done anything he wanted."

He chose to return to Chicago. He'd always planned to resume his community-building work in the city after law school—and had in fact promised colleagues at the DCP that he would return. But now he had another powerful reason for going back to Chicago: he was in love with a woman there.

LIFE PARTNER

Michelle Robinson grew up on Chicago's South Side in a tight-knit, working-class family. An excellent student, she earned a bachelor's degree in sociology from Princeton University before going on to Harvard Law School. After graduating from Harvard in 1988, she took a job as an associate with Sidley & Austin LLP, a large corporate law firm in Chicago. The following year, she was assigned to supervise a Harvard Law student the firm had hired as a summer intern. His name was Barack Obama.

The attraction, friends say, was immediate. Yet she initially rebuffed his efforts to see her socially, not wishing to become involved in an office romance. Obama persisted, however, and the two began dating. By 1991, when Obama returned to Chicago, they were engaged to be married.

The wedding took place in October 1992, at Trinity United Church of Christ. The joyous occasion was tinged with sadness. Michelle's father, Frasier Robinson, who

Like her husband, Michelle Obama is a graduate of Harvard Law School. Their family backgrounds, however, could hardly be more different. She grew up on Chicago's South Side in a two-parent, working-class black family. Friends say Michelle Obama is as strong-willed as her husband. He jokingly refers to her as one of the two higher powers he consults daily.

had long suffered from multiple sclerosis, had died earlier in the year, a few months before Stanley Dunham's death from prostate cancer. The groom, Obama's high school friend Greg Orme would recall, delivered a moving remembrance of his grandfather at the wedding reception. Gramps, Obama said, had "made a little boy with an absent father feel as though he was never alone."

AUTHOR, ACTIVIST, AND ATTORNEY

Obama had been quite busy over the previous year. He'd worked on *Dreams from My Father*, a book that would take several more years to complete. In April 1992 he'd taken a job as director of Illinois Project Vote, a voter registration and education campaign aimed at bringing low-income and minority Chicago-area residents into the electoral process. Obama hired and supervised a 10-person staff, and he directed a network of hundreds of volunteers. He also helped craft Project Vote's media effort. The slogan "It's a power thing" became familiar to Chicagoans through radio spots, printed materials, and even the T-shirts worn by Project Vote volunteers. The campaign ultimately succeeded in registering more than 150,000 new voters, most of them black, helping Democrat Carol Moseley Braun become the first African American woman elected to the U.S. Senate.

In 1993 Obama began work as an associate with Miner, Barnhill & Galland, P.C. The small Chicago firm, which specialized in civil rights law, couldn't offer Obama the high salary he would have commanded at a corporate law firm. But it did allow him to work on cases that fit his ideals.

Several of these cases involved voting rights. In one, Obama helped represent a community-organizing group in its lawsuit against the state of Illinois. The group contended

> **"[Obama] thinks issues through on their own merits, not through simple categories. He's most unusual in politics—someone whose own expertise, and sheer capacity for work and creative thought, outstrip those of policy specialists in many domains."**
>
> **—Cass Sunstein, professor of law and political science, University of Chicago**

that the state hadn't implemented a federal law intended to make it easier for poor people to register to vote. A federal court agreed, ordering Illinois to comply with the law. In another case, Obama helped represent African American aldermen and voters in Chicago, who charged that ward boundaries drawn up by city council after the 1990 census violated the Voting Rights Act by improperly diluting black voting power. Again, an appeals court agreed, and the boundaries were redrawn.

In addition to his work on voting rights issues, Obama took cases of employment discrimination. He also represented victims of housing discrimination.

In 1993, the same year he began practicing law at Miner, Barnhill & Galland, Obama began teaching law at the University of Chicago Law School. According to Cass Sunstein, who teaches political science and law at the University of Chicago, it was a conservative professor who first suggested that Obama be offered a position on the law school faculty. That professor, Michael McConnell, had been highly impressed by Obama's editing of an article McConnell had submitted to the *Harvard Law Review*. Obama was hired as a senior lecturer for the University of Chicago Law School. He taught courses on constitutional law, voting rights and the democratic process, and issues in racism and the law.

"Teaching keeps you sharp," Obama told the *New Yorker* magazine. "The great thing about teaching constitutional law is that all the tough questions land in your lap: abortion, gay rights, affirmative action. And you need to be able to argue both sides. . . . I think that's good for one's politics."

Colleagues at the University of Chicago Law School describe Obama as an excellent teacher, well respected for his legal knowledge and noteworthy for his ability to engage students. However, he never held a full-time, tenure-track position at the law school. That, colleagues say, was not because the school didn't want him as a permanent member of the faculty but because Obama declined the opportunity for tenure.

Although he enjoyed teaching, he didn't want a career in academia. Nor was he satisfied simply with practicing the law, which, he observed, sometimes seems like "a sort of glorified accounting that serves to regulate the affairs of those who have power—and that all too often seeks to explain, to those who do not, the ultimate wisdom and justness of their condition." He wanted to be an effective advocate for the poor and the powerless. And for some time he had been wondering whether the best way to accomplish that might be to enter politics.

SEEKING OFFICE

In August 1994 Mel Reynolds, a Democrat who represented Illinois's Second District in the U.S. House of Representatives, was indicted on charges stemming from an alleged sexual relationship with an underage girl. By the summer of 1995, as Reynolds's trial loomed, an Illinois state senator named Alice Palmer decided to oppose him in his bid for reelection the following year.

Palmer, a longtime community activist, was a highly respected African American Democrat who had represented the 13th District in the Illinois state senate since 1991. Politically, the 13th District—located in Chicago's South Side—was liberal and solidly Democratic. Socioeconomically, it was diverse, encompassing upscale neighborhoods around the University of Chicago in Hyde Park (where Barack and Michelle Obama had bought a condominium after their wedding); predominantly black middle- and working-class communities in South Shore (where Michelle Robinson Obama had grown up); and poverty-stricken African American communities in Englewood. Racially, the 13th District was majority black but contained significant numbers of whites.

When Palmer announced her run for Reynolds's seat in Congress, she informed influential Chicago Democrats that she would be giving up her seat in the state senate. But she heartily recommended a potential replacement with a stellar résumé: Ivy League college, Harvard Law, three years' experience as a South Side community organizer, civil rights attorney, lecturer in constitutional law.

In 1995 a criminal conviction forced three-term congressman Mel Reynolds (at right) to relinquish his seat in the U.S. House of Representatives. Reynolds's legal troubles helped open the way for Barack Obama to run for an Illinois state senate seat.

As Barack Obama's 34th birthday approached, circumstances could not have seemed more favorable for his long-contemplated move into politics. Obama was not one to leap right in, however. Exercising an abundance of caution, he asked Palmer whether she should consider filing to run for her state senate seat in addition to the seat in Congress. That way, if her congressional campaign didn't go well, she could drop out of the race and still keep her post as a state senator. Palmer assured Obama that, regardless of what happened in her run for the U.S. House of Representatives, she would not be returning to the Illinois legislature.

In July 1995, with Alice Palmer's blessing, Obama announced his intention to seek the office of state senator from the 13th District. He began doing all the things necessary for a successful political campaign: putting together a staff, organizing volunteers, leasing office space, raising money.

However, in early September 1995, after being convicted on multiple criminal charges, Mel Reynolds announced his resignation from Congress, effective October 1. A special election was called for November 28 so that Second District voters could choose a representative to serve the remaining year of Reynolds's term. In the abbreviated campaign, Alice Palmer lost badly to an opponent with a famous name: Jesse Jackson Jr., son of the African American civil rights advocate and two-time presidential candidate.

Within a couple weeks, Palmer had reconsidered her decision to give up her seat in the Illinois state senate. Facing a December 18 deadline, her supporters raced to collect the required number of voter signatures to put her name on the Democratic primary ballot the following March. And they quietly asked Barack Obama to shut down his fledgling campaign.

HARDBALL POLITICS

Obama found himself in a difficult position. Alice Palmer was considered an elder stateswoman of Chicago Democratic politics, and she was well liked by her colleagues at the State Capitol in Springfield. Palmer had powerful allies such as the South Side's Emil Jones Jr., minority leader of the Illinois senate. If Obama stepped aside, he would gain the goodwill of these influential Democrats, whose support could prove invaluable in future political endeavors. On the other hand, he was anxious to get into public office *now*. What's more, he'd already launched his campaign, and he seemed to be connecting well with 13th

Emil Jones Jr., a powerful Illinois Democrat, tried to get Obama to withdraw from the state senate race in favor of incumbent Alice Palmer. Obama refused.

District voters. After putting in a full workday at the law firm, Obama would head out each night to knock on doors and introduce himself to district residents. The former community organizer railed against corrupt politicians in Springfield, who, he said, put their careers before the common good, and he easily engaged people in conversations about the benefits of honest, responsive government. Obama, recalled campaign consultant Carol Anne Harwell, "would start a discussion that should have taken five minutes and pretty soon someone was cooking him dinner."

Although his campaign appeared to be making headway, a sober assessment of the situation had to give Obama pause. Palmer's reelection was a virtual certainty if he withdrew from the race, but she appeared to be a good bet to win even if he didn't. For a political novice like Obama, alienating powerful Democrats while still losing would be the worst outcome of all.

Aides recall that Obama agonized over what to do. In the end, however, he decided to stay in the race. Supporters of Palmer invited Obama to the home of a state representative in an effort to change his mind. Obama accepted the invitation and went to the meeting alone. Timuel Black, a university professor and Palmer supporter who was present at the meeting, recalled that Obama stood his ground. "He did not put it in inflammatory terms," Black said, "he just did not back away. It was not arguments, it was stubbornness. Barack had by then gone ahead in putting together his own campaign, and he just didn't want to stop."

Obama sounded a bit testy on December 18, the deadline for submitting nominating petitions. He blasted Palmer for trying to pressure him to drop out of the race and told newspaper reporters, "I am disappointed that she's decided to go back on her word to me."

The stage seemed set for a dramatic primary race pitting a popular veteran politician against a bright newcomer. But Alice Palmer's campaign would barely survive past New Year's. On January 2, when the candidates presented their nominating petitions to the election board at Chicago's city hall, Obama had a crack team on hand to challenge the validity of Palmer's petitions—as well as those of his three other opponents in the Democratic field. In hearings that lasted a week, Obama's team—led by Harvard-trained lawyer Tom Johnson—had name after name stricken from the other candidates' nominating petitions. In some instances, signatures had apparently been forged; in others, petition circulators hadn't followed legally mandated procedures. In still other cases, people who signed the nominating petitions of Obama's opponents had recently been purged from the voter rolls.

At the conclusion of the nominating-petition hearings, Barack Obama was the only Democratic candidate with enough voter signatures to get on the ballot. Challenging the validity of nominating petitions is a perfectly legal—and, in Chicago, widely used—tactic, but Obama's actions rankled some. His work for Project Vote had been about pulling more people into the political process, but now the slogan "It's a power thing" seemed to take on new meaning. "Why say you're for a new tomorrow," complained Gha-is

> ## Obama on Obama
>
> " I'm somebody who generally thinks that listening and learning before you start talking is a pretty good strategy. "

Askia, one of the candidates eliminated by Obama's petition challenges, "then do old-style Chicago politics to remove legitimate candidates? . . . Why not let the people decide?"

Interviewed years later, Obama conceded that "there's a legitimate argument to be made that you shouldn't create barriers to people getting on the ballot." However, he defended his tactics. "To my mind," he said, "we were just abiding by the rules that had been set up. I gave some thought to . . . should people be on the ballot even if they didn't meet the requirements. My conclusion was that if you couldn't run a successful petition drive, then that raised questions in terms of how effective a representative you were going to be."

In any event, Obama ran unopposed in the Democratic primary in March. In November he easily defeated his Republican rival in the heavily Democratic district. At 36, Obama had gained his first elected office.

Chapter 8 LEGISLATIVE LESSONS

*I*n January 1997, when Obama arrived in Springfield to begin his legislative career, he understood the limits on what he would be able to accomplish. At the time, the General Assembly of Illinois was dominated by Republicans. As a freshman senator from the minority party, Obama would have no chance of enacting the sweeping progressive agenda he favored. In fact, it was unlikely that any bill he authored would even get out of committee.

But Obama faced an unexpected obstacle at the Capitol as well. He quickly discovered that many of his new colleagues—including fellow Democrats—resented him. During his campaign, Obama had decried the corrupt practices of the General Assembly, which certainly didn't make him many friends in Springfield. Some fellow legislators were also put off by his reputation as a top-notch legal mind—and by what they regarded as his condescending attitude. They chafed at the idea that this University of Chicago Law School lecturer with the fancy Harvard degree thought he knew more than they did about how to do the public's business.

And then there were some legislators, especially in the Senate Black Caucus, who didn't like the way Obama had unseated Alice Palmer. A few belittled him for what they saw as his privileged background, and especially for the ease with which he moved in elite—and white—circles. These members would "just give Barack hell," recalled Kimberly Lightford, who at the time was the chair of the Senate Black Caucus. One, Senator Donne Trotter, would tell a Chicago newspaper, "Barack is viewed in part to be the white man in blackface in our community."

Obama worked hard to change the perceptions senate colleagues had of him. He joined them in pickup basketball games and in golf outings. He attended cocktail parties in the Capitol with his colleagues and lobbyists. He became a regular at "the Committee Meeting," as legislators and lobbyists dubbed their long-running Wednesday night poker game. All of this helped alter the image of Obama as a stuck-up intellectual. "When it turned out that I could sit down at [a bar] and have a beer and watch a game or go out for a round of golf or get a poker game going," he recalled, "I probably confounded some of their expectations."

BUILDING BRIDGES

In the legislative chamber, Obama moved cautiously. He sought out Emil Jones, who had tried to prevent him from unseating Alice Palmer, and made it a point to tell Jones that he wanted to work with him. The senate minority leader responded to this overture by giving the freshman important assignments. For example, he assigned Obama the delicate task of spearheading ethics reform in the senate, and he tapped Obama to lead negotiations with Republicans over welfare reform legislation.

Typically, such assignments go to legislators with more seniority, and some Democrats grumbled about what they considered the minority leader's special treatment of Obama. Asked years later to explain his relationship with the freshman lawmaker, Jones said that he saw in Obama a person whose extraordinary gifts might one day enable him to accomplish all the things that Jones himself had spent his life working for.

Kirk Dillard, a powerful Republican senator from the Chicago suburbs, offered a similar assessment of Obama. "I knew from the day he walked into this chamber,"

Obama confers with Emil Jones. When he arrived in Springfield in 1997, Obama reached out to the veteran lawmaker— with whom he had tangled during his campaign. Jones, who was then the Illinois senate minority leader, responded by giving Obama important assignments.

Dillard said, "that he was destined for great things. In Republican circles, we've always feared that Barack would become a rock star of American politics."

Other colleagues insist it was apparent to them very early on that Obama's political ambitions extended well beyond the Illinois legislature. One veteran Democrat recalled how Obama, with only months under his belt in

Obama jokes with Illinois state senate colleagues Kirk Dillard (left) and Don Harmon. Initially, Obama faced considerable resentment from fellow lawmakers in Springfield. But he gradually won over colleagues with his cordiality, diligence, and ability to work with Republicans.

the senate, invited him out for a beer and picked his brain about how Obama might fare in a statewide race.

Higher ambitions or not, Obama emerged as a leader in the Illinois senate. Colleagues' descriptions of his style—methodical, inclusive, pragmatic—echoed the descriptions of people who worked with him during his years as a community organizer and during his tenure as president of the *Harvard Law Review*.

In the Illinois senate, some liberal Democrats were prone to unleashing incendiary rhetoric against the Republicans who blocked the programs they favored. Obama saw such histrionics as not only disagreeable but also pointless. Demonizing political opponents, he believed, achieved nothing. A more effective way to legislate was to seek areas of agreement in a civil manner. Politics is, after all, the art of compromise. "You can't always come up with the optimal solution," Obama told *New Yorker* magazine writer William Finnegan, "but you can usually come up with a better solution. A good compromise, a good piece of legislation, is like a good sentence."

Obama worked diligently with Republicans on bipartisan measures. He played a key role in drafting ethics legislation. He succeeded in enlisting Republican support for measures designed to ensure that the death penalty (which he supported for certain crimes) was applied equitably, without regard for the defendant's race and class. He also worked with Republicans to pass legislation to make it less likely that Illinois would execute an innocent person.

"He was passionate in his views," recalled Dave Syverson, a Republican who worked with Obama on

> **To be young, black and brilliant has always appeared to me to be one of the more extraordinary burdens in American life. Much is offered; even more is expected. You are like a walking Statue of Liberty, holding up the torch 24 hours a day. Yet Barack Obama . . . is in every sense comfortable in his own skin and committed to a political vision far broader than racial categories.**
>
> **—Scott Turow, writer and lawyer**

> ### Obama on Obama
>
> " I think that the reason I got into politics was simply because I saw the law as being inadequate to the task. It's very difficult to bring about social change at this point through the courts. [And] community organizing was too localized and too small. "

welfare reform legislation. "We had some pretty fierce arguments. We went round and round about how much to spend on day care, for example. But he was not your typical party-line politician. A lot of Democrats didn't want to have any work requirement at all for people on welfare. Barack was willing to make that deal."

Obama cared deeply about issues affecting the poor and disadvantaged. If the laws that were ultimately passed didn't contain everything he might have wanted, he believed they represented steps in the right direction. And they testified to Obama's willingness and ability to find common ground with people holding different views. "He's not dogmatic," Emil Jones noted, "he's consensus building."

"Obama," Kirk Dillard remarked, "is an extraordinary man. . . . He's to the left of me on gun control, abortion. But he can really work with Republicans."

"A Good Spanking"

In 1999 Barack and Michelle Obama welcomed their first child, a daughter they named Malia. The new father set his sights on a new job as well.

Against the advice of friends in the state senate, Obama had decided to seek a seat in the U.S. House of Representatives. He would challenge Bobby Rush, a four-term congressman from Illinois's First District—which included the South Side of Chicago—in the Democratic primary in 2000.

Rush, a former Black Panther and community activist, was much better known than his opponent, and Obama's campaign never really got untracked. Obama solicited the help of the church pastors with whom he had worked as a community organizer. He pounded the streets, speaking with anyone who would listen. He made seemingly endless phone calls seeking campaign donations. But the response was lukewarm. Rush had deep roots in the communities he represented, and most people saw no reason he shouldn't return to Washington for another term.

The campaign got ugly, and Obama found himself on the receiving end of stinging personal attacks. He was called an arrogant elitist. Some critics said he wasn't black enough to represent the South Side. Obama tried to defend himself against these charges. "When Congressman Rush and his allies attack me for going to Harvard and teaching at the University of Chicago," he said on one occasion, "they're sending a signal to black kids that if you're

Bobby Rush was a popular four-term U.S. congressman representing the First District in Illinois when Barack Obama decided to challenge him in the 2000 Democratic primary. Obama received a beating at the ballot box.

well-educated, somehow you're not 'keeping it real.' " But, campaign observers suggested, the charges of Obama's critics resonated with many voters. Obama seemed unprepared for the rough-and-tumble fight, and throughout the campaign he gave the impression of being aloof.

By the time Election Day arrived, Obama knew he was going to lose. He stood outside polling places, shaking hands, smiling, and asking for the support of voters as they arrived to cast their ballots. Mostly they smiled and walked past him, but some voters told Obama that while he seemed like a nice enough fellow, "Bobby ain't done nothing wrong."

Rush's victory in the Democratic primary was overwhelming. The popular incumbent garnered 61 percent of the vote to Obama's 30 percent. "I got a good spanking," Obama recalled.

FAMILY MATTERS

Colleagues in the Illinois senate describe Obama as humbled by his defeat. Yet, with Republicans still in control of the chamber, he redoubled his efforts to advance a progressive agenda. He pushed for tax credits for the state's working poor. He authored legislation that gave 20,000 more children coverage under Illinois's health insurance system, and he laid out a plan to provide health insurance for all children.

Obama soon had another child of his own. In 2001 Michelle gave birth to their second daughter, Sasha. Juggling a busy legislative schedule and family obligations was often difficult for Obama. Michelle, who had a high-powered career of her own at the University of Chicago, took on the lion's share of the added workload. But she insisted that her husband do his part and remain a visible father. Her recriminations could be stinging. In his book *The*

Michelle and Barack Obama with their daughters, Sasha (left) and Malia.
Throughout his career in politics, Michelle Obama has insisted that her husband
balance work and family obligations.

Audacity of Hope, Obama wrote that when he was spending too much time at work, Michelle would complain, "I never thought I'd have to raise a family alone." She had grown up in a solid family and knew how important that was to her children. Barack Obama, too, knew how important it was for him to be around, although for different reasons.

Obama ran for reelection in 2002 without opposition. This allowed him to focus on matters beyond the Illinois legislature. He turned his attention to national issues and to the growing prospect of war.

DRUMBEAT TO WAR

On the morning of September 11, 2001, Islamic terrorists hijacked four U.S. commercial jets. The terrorists flew two of the jets into the twin towers of New York City's World Trade Center and another into the Pentagon, outside Washington, D.C. The fourth jet crashed into a field in western Pennsylvania after a struggle between passengers and the hijackers. The loss of life was appalling: some 3,000 people were killed in the coordinated attacks, the worst terrorist incident ever on U.S. soil.

It quickly became apparent that an organization named al-Qaeda ("the Base") was responsible for the September 11 attacks. Established and led by a wealthy Saudi exile named Osama bin Laden, al-Qaeda aimed to rid the Middle East of Western influence and to replace the region's governments—which it considered corrupt and

Smoke rises from the Pentagon, outside Washington, D.C., on the night of September 11, 2001. Earlier in the day, terrorists sponsored by a radical Islamist group called al-Qaeda had crashed four hijacked jetliners. About 3,000 people lost their lives in the terrorist attacks.

impious—with conservative Islamic regimes. Bin Laden particularly despised the United States, and he told followers that is was their duty to kill Americans, even civilians.

Bin Laden and al-Qaeda were operating out of Afghanistan, where they had established training bases and where they were guests of the country's Taliban government. Following the September 11 attacks, U.S. president George W. Bush demanded that the Taliban—an extreme Islamic fundamentalist regime—turn over bin Laden and his al-Qaeda associates to face justice. The Taliban refused.

In October 2001, U.S. military forces invaded Afghanistan and, joined by Afghan rebels, quickly toppled the Taliban government. Bin Laden was chased into the rugged mountains of Tora Bora, in eastern Afghanistan near the Pakistan border. He appeared to be cornered there, but bin Laden managed to escape into Pakistan, where he disappeared.

Almost immediately, the Bush administration turned its attention to another country in the region: Iraq. Over the ensuing months, administration officials began to make a case for war with Iraq. They said that Iraq supported al-Qaeda and was harboring terrorists from the group. Some officials went a step further and attempted to link Iraq directly with the September 11 attacks, claiming that an Iraqi government agent had met with one of the hijackers in Prague, the capital of the Czech Republic. Administration officials said that Iraq had stockpiles of chemical and biological weapons, which it might use against Americans or turn over to terrorists intent on attacking the United States. The Bush administration even raised the specter of an Iraq-sponsored nuclear attack on the United States—saying that the nation could not afford to wait until a mushroom cloud rose over an American city before taking action.

No one could deny that Iraq's president, Saddam Hussein, was a ruthless dictator whose ambitions had caused enormous suffering in Iraq and in neighboring countries. In 1980 Saddam had ordered the invasion of Iran, touching off an eight-year war that claimed a million or more casualties in the two countries. During that war and in its aftermath, Iraqi forces had used chemical weapons—which are banned by the Geneva Conventions— against Iranian troops and against Iraqi Kurds suspected of siding with Iran. In 1990 Saddam had ordered the invasion of Kuwait.

The following year, after Iraqi forces had been expelled from Kuwait by a U.S.-led international coalition, Saddam had been forced to accept as a condition of peace that his country dismantle its weapons of mass destruction (WMD) programs and destroy all stockpiled WMD. (WMD include chemical, biological, and nuclear weapons.) To ensure Iraqi compliance, United Nations weapons inspectors were dispatched to Iraq.

Years of UN weapons inspections had uncovered and destroyed stockpiles of chemical and biological weapons. But Iraq had continually tried to thwart the inspectors, and the Bush administration—along with the vast majority of foreign governments and intelligence experts—believed that this was because Saddam had something to hide.

By the fall of 2002, President Bush was arguing that the United States might have to launch a preemptive war against Iraq to prevent another attack on the United States. A large majority of Americans supported this course of action (opinion polling by the Pew Charitable Trusts found 64 percent of Americans in favor of an invasion of Iraq as of September 19). Most elected officials also lined up behind the policy of the popular president.

On October 11, the U.S. Senate would vote 77-23 to authorize the use of force against Iraq; all but one Republican and the majority of Democrats voted in favor of giving the president the go-ahead for war.

PROFILE IN COURAGE

It was in this context—with fear, patriotic fervor, and a popular president leading the country toward what seemed an inevitable war—that Barack Obama appeared before an antiwar rally in Chicago. The date was October 2, 2002, five months before the U.S. invasion.

In October 2002 a joint resolution giving President George W. Bush authorization to use force against Iraq passed Congress overwhelmingly. In the Senate, as this video still shows, the vote was 77-23. In the House of Representatives, the resolution passed by a margin of 296-133.

When he arrived at the rally, Obama noticed many people wearing buttons with the slogan "War Is Not an Option." "I don't agree with that," he recalled thinking. "Sometimes war is an option." He made that the subject of his remarks:

> I stand before you as someone who is not opposed to war in all circumstances. The Civil War was one of the bloodiest in history, and yet it was only through the crucible of the sword, the sacrifice of multitudes, that we could begin to perfect this union, and drive the scourge of slavery from our soil. I don't oppose all wars.
>
> My grandfather signed up for a war the day after Pearl Harbor was bombed, [and] fought in Patton's army. . . . He fought in the name of a larger freedom, part of that arsenal of democracy that triumphed over evil, and he did not fight in vain. I don't oppose all wars.
>
> After September 11th, after witnessing the carnage and destruction, the dust and the tears, I supported this administration's pledge to hunt down and root out those who would slaughter innocents in the name of intolerance, and I would willingly take up arms myself to prevent such tragedy from happening again. I don't oppose all wars. And I know that in this crowd today, there is no shortage of patriots, or of patriotism.
>
> What I am opposed to is a dumb war. What I am opposed to is a rash war. What I am opposed to is the cynical attempt by . . . armchair, weekend warriors in this administration to shove their own ideological agendas down our throats, irrespective of the costs in lives lost and in hardships borne.
>
> . . . That's what I'm opposed to. . . . A war based not on reason but on passion, not on principle but on politics.

The "War Is Not an Option" types might not have agreed with what Obama said. Yet it was precisely what many opponents of George Bush's Iraq policy had been longing to hear: not platitudes or pie-in-the-sky pacifism, but a clear-eyed opposition to *this* war as an ill-advised affront to justice. They would not hear that message from the Democratic Party's national leaders—not from Senate Majority Leader Tom Daschle; not from John Kerry, John Edwards, or Joe Lieberman, who would seek their party's presidential nomination in 2004; not from Hillary Clinton or Joe Biden, who would run for president in 2008. All of these politicians voted to give the president the authority to go to war against Iraq.

Obama—young, charismatic, and eloquent—reminded some older people at the antiwar rally of another politician from another turbulent time in American history. In 1968 Robert Kennedy had spoken out forcefully against the Vietnam War.

As Obama continued his speech, he warned of the dire consequences a U.S. invasion of Iraq would produce.

> Now let me be clear—I suffer no illusions about Saddam Hussein. He is a brutal man. A ruthless man. A man who butchers his own people to secure his own power. . . . The world, and the Iraqi people, would be better off without him.
>
> But I also know that Saddam poses no imminent and direct threat to the United States, or to his neighbors . . . and that in concert with the international community he can be contained until, in the way of all petty dictators, he falls away into the dustbin of history. I know that even a successful war against Iraq will require a US occupation of undetermined length, at undetermined cost, with

undetermined consequences. I know that an invasion of Iraq without a clear rationale and without
strong international support will only fan the flames
of the Middle East, and encourage the worst, rather
than best, impulses of the Arab world, and
strengthen the recruitment arm of al-Qaeda.

The Bush administration was predicting an easy victory
in Iraq. Iraqis, the administration insisted, would welcome
American troops as liberators, and U.S. forces would be
able to withdraw quickly, leaving in place a democratic
government that would be a beacon of hope for the
Middle East.

Many Middle East scholars, and many military and foreign policy professionals, were skeptical of this rosy sce-
nario. But their voices were generally ignored or shouted
down in the run-up to the war. Barack Obama went on
record opposing the war when it was politically risky to do
so. And, whereas the Bush administration's predictions
about the conflict turned out to be tragically wrong—and
its justifications for the war were shown to be largely without foundation—the state senator from Illinois was spot-on
in his judgment.

Chapter 9 MR. OBAMA GOES TO WASHINGTON

B arack Obama's party fared very well in the 2002 state elections in Illinois. When the General Assembly convened early the following year, Democrats were in control of the legislature for the first time since Obama had arrived in Springfield.

This meant that Obama would have a greater chance to pass the kinds of laws he believed would be good for the people of Illinois. He seized the opportunity.

As the new chairman of the Senate Health and Human Services Committee, Obama worked to pass legislation supporting residents of the state who could not afford health insurance. He helped pass bills to increase funding for AIDS prevention and care programs.

In an effort to reduce the chances that a coerced confession might lead to a wrongful execution, Obama authored a bill requiring police to videotape formal interviews with, and confessions of, murder suspects. Over objections from the law enforcement community, he succeeded in getting the bill passed. It was the first law of its kind in the United States.

Obama also secured the passage of a landmark bill aimed at ending racial profiling, a law enforcement practice by which, critics charged, African Americans were unfairly singled out for scrutiny and harassment. The bill required that Illinois police officers record the race of drivers in all the traffic stops they made.

In addition, Obama was again at the forefront of ethics reform efforts. The legislation he helped pass in 2003 included restrictions on the gifts lawmakers could accept from lobbyists. It also authorized the appointment of inspectors to root out corruption in state agencies.

LOOKING AHEAD

If Democratic control of the General Assembly gave Barack Obama a chance to get his progressive agenda enacted, it afforded him other opportunities as well. Emil Jones, who became the Illinois senate president by virtue of the Democrats' electoral victory in 2002, recalls Obama visiting him in his office one day and telling him, "You're a very powerful guy." Jones asked why that was, and Obama replied, "You could help elect a U.S. senator." When Jones asked if Obama had anyone in mind, he was told, "Yeah. Me."

Obama had decided to challenge Peter Fitzgerald, a Republican who was up for reelection in 2004. In January 2003, with the primary elections more than a year away, Obama formally announced his candidacy.

Other candidates decided to enter the race after Fitzgerald announced, in April, that he'd decided not to seek reelection. Obama was considered an underdog in the crowded Democratic primary field.

When Republican Peter Fitzgerald declared in April 2003 that he would not seek reelection to the U.S. Senate, a host of candidates entered the race to succeed him.

Among the half-dozen other candidates, the frontrunner was Blair Hull, a multimillionaire businessman who plunged $29 million into his campaign. Dan Hynes, the comptroller of the state, was also formidable; he enjoyed the backing of much of the Chicago Democratic Party as well as the labor unions.

Illinois is a big state with great diversity. Chicago, the third-largest city in the United States, is one of the nation's great metropolises but has all the problems of other urban areas. Downstate Illinois is largely agricultural and rural. The two regions have little in common.

To win the Senate race, Obama knew that he would have to carry Chicago big and keep his losses in the rural downstate areas to a minimum. This would be the first time in his political career that Obama faced rural voters,

African Americans in the Senate

Since Reconstruction ended in 1877, there have been just three black members of the United States Senate. They are:

Edward Brooke (R-Massachusetts), 1967–1979.
Carol Moseley Braun (D-Illinois), 1993–1999.
Barack Obama (D-Illinois), 2005–.

and he wasn't sure how they would respond to a black man who lived in Chicago. But Obama was determined to campaign hard downstate. He believed that he knew the people there, for they weren't so different from the mother and grandparents who had raised him. People from rural Kansas and rural Illinois shared the same values of the Midwest: honesty, self-reliance, hard work. Obama knew their manners and their sensibilities; they were the manners and sensibilities he was taught growing up.

Pundits who had assumed Obama would be uncomfortable campaigning in the white, rural areas of Illinois were soon proved wrong. Farmers and other downstate residents warmed up to him. Often, Obama would start a speech by making light of his unusual name. People were always calling him "Alabama" or "Yo' Mama," he would say. Then he would segue into a discussion of race, community, and common values. At a rally in Decatur, for example, he told the crowd, "We have shared values, values that aren't black or white or Hispanic—values that are American, and Democratic." Obama then proceeded to explain why he was running for the Senate: "People are always asking me, 'Why, with these fancy degrees and a professorship, would you want to go into something dirty and nasty like politics?'

And my answer is 'We've got too much cynicism in this country, and we're all in this together, and government expresses that.' "

As Obama introduced himself to people throughout the state of Illinois, one of his supporters brought his name to the attention of President Bush. Jan Schakowsky, a Democrat who represents Illinois's Ninth District in the U.S. House of Representatives, was visiting the White House with a congressional delegation when the president noticed the "OBAMA" button she

Obama and Illinois comptroller Dan Hynes share a light moment at a debate among Democratic contenders for the U.S. Senate, January 2004. In March, after the candidacy of millionaire businessman Blair Hull foundered on allegations of domestic abuse, Obama decisively defeated Hynes and the rest of the Democratic field.

was wearing. "He jumped back, almost literally," Schakowsky told *New Yorker* magazine writer William Finnegan. "And I knew what he was thinking. So I reassured him it was Obama, with a 'b.' And I explained who he was. The President said, 'Well, *I* don't know him.' So I just said, 'You will.' "

CATCHING A BREAK

Obama's campaign got a major break when allegations of domestic abuse surfaced against Blair Hull. As Hull's candidacy tanked, the race came down to Obama and Dan Hynes. During the last few weeks of the campaign, Obama surged. He garnered public support from Sheila Simon, the daughter of one of downstate Illinois's most popular and respected figures: former U.S. senator Paul Simon, who had died the previous December. Obama also won endorsements from both major Chicago newspapers, the *Tribune* and the *Sun-Times*.

On March 16, 2004, Democratic voters went to the polls and gave Barack Obama a decisive primary win. Obama received 52 percent of the vote, more than double that of his nearest rival, Hynes. "I am fired up!" Obama told supporters at his victory celebration.

> I think it's fair to say the conventional wisdom was we could not win. We did not have enough money. We did not have enough organization. There was no way that a skinny guy from the South Side [of Chicago] with a funny name like "Barack Obama" could win a statewide race. Sixteen months later we are here, and Democrats all across Illinois—suburbs, city, downstate, upstate, Black, White, Hispanic, Asian—have declared, "Yes, we can! Yes, we can!"

Obama celebrates his U.S. Senate primary victory with his family and supporters.

A RIVAL FALLS

Despite this enthusiasm, Obama still had much work to do before he could claim the Senate seat. Republican primary voters had chosen a formidable candidate: millionaire Jack Ryan. Ryan, like Obama, had an Ivy League undergraduate education and a law degree from Harvard. He also held a master's degree in business administration from Harvard Business School. In 2000 Ryan left a prestigious and high-paying job at the investment bank Goldman Sachs to teach at an all-black high school on Chicago's South Side.

But Ryan, it turned out, also had some personal baggage. During divorce proceedings several years earlier, his ex-wife, Jeri, had made embarrassing sexual allegations against him. Those allegations became public in June 2004, after Chicago media outlets successfully sued to have court

119

records from the Ryans' divorce unsealed. On June 25, Ryan was forced to withdraw from the Senate race.

Meanwhile, Obama's campaign gained momentum. His keynote speech to the Democratic National Convention made him one of the nation's most talked-about political figures.

OBAMA VS. KEYES

The Illinois Republican Party scrambled to recruit a replacement candidate to run against Obama. Finally, on August 8, Alan Keyes agreed to carry the Republican banner. An African American from Maryland (to become eligible for elective office in Illinois, he had to move to the state before the election), Keyes was no stranger to the spotlight. Through his books, a syndicated radio program,

Obama makes a point during his third and final televised debate with Alan Keyes, October 26, 2004. One week later, Obama routed Keyes at the polls, recording the largest margin of victory in any U.S. Senate race in Illinois history.

and a short-lived cable TV talk show, he had gained prominence as a spokesperson for conservative values. Twice he had been the Republican nominee for a U.S. Senate seat from Maryland, losing both times in the general election; twice he had unsuccessfully pursued his party's presidential nomination.

Obama and Keyes faced off in three televised debates. On a range of social, economic, and foreign-policy issues, the two candidates expressed opposing views. Obama supported stem cell research, which Keyes opposed. Obama supported abortion rights; Keyes was solidly pro-life. Obama was against tax cuts that he said would benefit the wealthy; Keyes favored abolishing the income tax altogether. Obama supported gun control, while Keyes opposed it. Keyes insisted that President Bush's decision to invade Iraq had been correct, whereas Obama characterized the war as a terrible strategic blunder.

But the campaign was not exclusively about the issues. In fact, some observers accused Keyes of straying into personal attacks against his opponent. For example, he labeled Obama a "hard-line, academic Marxist." A Catholic, Keyes also injected religion into the campaign. He told an interviewer that "people of Catholic conscience—not only Catholic conscience, people of Christian conscience—I don't see how they could vote for Barack Obama." He even asserted that "Christ would not vote for Barack Obama."

Obama didn't respond in kind to these attacks. Instead he answered Keyes's calls for a return to "Christian principles" with a plea of his own: be tolerant of other people's religious beliefs, so long as those beliefs don't cause anyone harm or impinge on another's right to believe differently.

Part of the explanation for Obama's refusal to resort to negative campaigning might be that he had that luxury:

polls showed him well ahead of his Republican opponent. But Obama also claimed that he wanted to create a new kind of politics. Negative campaigning, he has said, makes people cynical. Over time voters become turned off to politics and stop paying attention. This allows special interests space to pursue their agendas, frequently to the detriment of the American people as a whole.

On November 2, 2004, Illinois voters went to the polls and gave Obama a huge endorsement. Obama received 70 percent of the vote to Keyes's 27 percent. It was the widest margin of victory in any U.S. Senate race in Illinois history. Some hailed it as a victory over cynicism.

JUNIOR SENATOR FROM ILLINOIS

On January 4, 2005, Barack Obama was sworn in as a United States senator. He was surrounded by guests from Hawaii, London, Kenya, and Indonesia. Michelle was there, of course, along with the Obamas' daughters, Malia and Sasha. His sister Maya was there with her Canadian-Chinese husband. So was his sister Auma. Ann Dunham didn't witness her son's triumphant moment; she had died of ovarian cancer in 1995. But Toot flew in from Hawaii. The scene bore a vague resemblance to a meeting of the United Nations.

For a freshman senator, Obama put together an unusually experienced and high-powered staff. His chief of staff, Pete Rouse, had previously served in the same capacity for Tom Daschle, the former Senate Democratic leader. Obama also hired an economist who had been deputy chief of staff to Secretary of the Treasury Robert Rubin. He chose Samantha Power, a Harvard lecturer and Pulitzer Prize–winning author, as his foreign-policy adviser.

Among many rank-and-file Democrats, expectations of what Obama could accomplish were ridiculously high. In part this was because of his rousing keynote address at the Democratic National Convention, in part because his victory was one of the few bright spots for the Democratic Party in the 2004 elections. Those elections had seen Republican incumbent George W. Bush defeat Democrat John Kerry for the presidency. Republicans had gained four seats in the Senate, giving them a 55-44 majority in the upper chamber of Congress (the Senate also had one independent member). In addition, the Republicans had picked up seats in

The Obamas with Vice President Dick Cheney after the swearing-in ceremony for the U.S. Senate, January 4, 2005.

Obama on Obama

"

I have good instincts about big-picture politics. I'm not a political mechanic. There are a lot of people who are a lot smarter when it comes to press turnout, polling, or what have you. . . . But in terms of what's important to the country and what's important to people, I think my instincts are good. I trust them.

"

the House of Representatives and enjoyed a comfortable working majority in that chamber as well.

Obama entered the Senate ranking 99th out of 100 in seniority. Moreover, his party was in the minority. As had been the case when he arrived in Springfield as a freshman state senator, there would clearly be limits on what he could get done in the 109th Congress.

Obama said he needed time to learn how the Senate worked and to build relationships with more experienced colleagues. "I'm feeling very much like the rookie and looking for guidance from those who've been there for 15 or 20 years," he explained.

Obama may have wanted to keep a low profile, but the media spotlight was intense and unrelenting. Even before his swearing-in ceremony, Obama had joked, "I'm so overexposed I make Paris Hilton look like a recluse." With the United States at war, his Senate committee assignments—Foreign Relations; Veterans' Affairs; Homeland Security and Governmental Affairs—ensured him a fair degree of visibility. (Obama was also assigned to the Senate Health, Education, Labor, and Pensions Committee.)

Veterans' issues would be among the first matters Senator Obama tackled. After it came to light that the federal government was paying disabled veterans in six states—including Illinois—considerably less than disabled vets in other states, Obama and fellow Democrat Dick Durbin, the senior senator from Illinois, set up hearings to investigate the situation. Obama then cosponsored legislation permitting veterans to seek redress.

OF WAR AND PEACE

For someone who had criticized the Iraq War so vocally, Obama was notably quiet on the subject throughout most of his first year in the Senate. In November 2005 he gave a

Senators Daniel Akaka (D-Hawaii) and Barack Obama chat with members of the U.S. armed forces after a hearing by the Senate Committee on Veterans' Affairs. Obama has been a vocal champion of better health care and disability benefits for veterans.

speech calling for a reduction in the number of American soldiers in Iraq. But, significantly, he did not advocate a timetable for U.S. withdrawal from Iraq—a position that had already been articulated by a few Democratic legislators. And, in June of 2006, he voted against an amendment that would have mandated a troop-withdrawal timetable.

Obama's tepid stance disappointed many antiwar activists. But he insisted that precipitous action would have destroyed the chances of a stable government taking root in Iraq. "At the time, my view was that the [Iraqi] government was still forming," Obama stated, "and it would be important to not give the impression, prior to the formation of that government, that we were already on the way out."

Obama explained that after the situation in Iraq devolved into civil war, it made sense to change U.S. policy. In January 2007 he introduced the Iraq War De-Escalation Act of 2007. It called for capping the number of American troops in Iraq at January 2007 levels, then beginning a phased redeployment with the goal of removing all combat forces from Iraq by March 31, 2008. The language of Obama's bill was consistent with the recommendations of the Iraq Study Group, a blue-ribbon, bipartisan panel whose long-awaited report was issued in December 2006.

A STUDENT OF FOREIGN POLICY

Obama came to Washington with no experience in foreign policy. But, according to aides and colleagues, he worked extremely hard to educate himself. His capacity to synthesize information from many sources, and his intuitive ability to see connections and grasp implications, sometimes astounded people with long experience in international relations. "He's a sponge," Samantha Power, Obama's foreign-policy adviser, said. "He pushes so hard on policy ideas that fifteen minutes after you've started talking, he's sent you back to the drawing board."

In addition to his tutelage by Power, Obama sought out a Republican colleague, Richard Lugar of Indiana. Lugar—at the time chairman of the Senate Foreign Relations Committee—is one of Washington's most respected voices in international affairs. Obama traveled with Lugar to Eastern Europe and Russia on a fact-finding mission to gauge the progress of programs designed to secure nuclear weapons materials in the former Soviet Union. Later the two collaborated on a bill to keep terrorists from gaining access to stockpiles of conventional weapons, such as shoulder-fired missiles and anti-personnel mines.

Senator Richard Lugar (R-Indiana) has worked with Obama on a range of issues, including nuclear nonproliferation, the securing of conventional-weapons stockpiles, increased fuel efficiency standards in the United States, and the promotion of renewable energy sources. Obama, Lugar says, has "a sense of idealism and principled leadership, a vision of the future."

Obama concluded that future threats to American security won't come primarily from traditional sources—that is, other powerful states and their militaries. Rather, these threats will come from weak and impoverished states and states where order has broken down. In Obama's view, these societies have the potential to incubate problems that, in an era of globalization, can easily spread to American shores. For example, countries with poor or nonexistent public health systems are unlikely to contain outbreaks of infectious disease within their borders. A deadly strain of influenza might arise in, say, Vietnam, but a few infected airline passengers could quickly spread it around the world. Similarly, extreme poverty and conflict in a foreign country might not pose an immediate threat to America, but those conditions can produce failed states (states that lack a governing authority capable of performing essential functions such as security). In such places terrorists can easily find room to operate: Osama bin Laden, for instance, established his successive headquarters in two failed states, Sudan and Afghanistan. Moreover, grievances born of poverty, injustice, and hopelessness can breed radicalism.

Obama's worldview, his advisers have noted, starts with a recognition of the growing interconnectedness of the globe's countries and peoples. What happens in distant countries—even those that are impoverished and without significant military power—can threaten the security of the United States. Thus, promoting the welfare of people stricken by poverty, oppression, and violence—in addition to being morally right—is in America's self-interest and, Obama believes, must occupy a larger focus of U.S. foreign policy.

This philosophy was evident in the first piece of legislation of which Obama was the primary sponsor. The

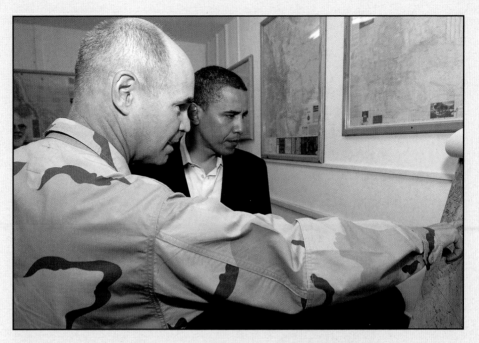

Senator Barack Obama receives a briefing from Rear Admiral Richard Hunt, commander of the Combined Joint Task Force–Horn of Africa (CJTF–HOA), Djibouti, August 2006. In addition to conducting operations to disrupt terrorist networks, CJTF–HOA assists regional states with humanitarian support. Obama, who takes a holistic view of foreign affairs, believes that the United States cannot afford to ignore problems such as poverty and political disorder in developing countries.

Democratic Republic of Congo Relief, Security, and Democracy Promotion Act—which President Bush signed into law on December 22, 2006—aimed to help end the long-running conflict and alleviate the humanitarian catastrophe in the huge African country. Obama was also a prominent advocate for using U.S. influence to end another horrendous conflict in Africa—the fighting in Sudan's western Darfur region. Obama cosponsored all major Senate legislation aimed at protecting the civilian victims of that conflict, earning him an A+ rating from the Washington-based group Genocide Intervention Network.

Ideally, however, a more proactive American foreign policy approach could avert crises. "By investing now," Obama observed, "we avoid an Iraq or Afghanistan later."

Obama's approach has won praise from his Republican colleague Richard Lugar. "My comment is not meant to be unkind to mainstream Democrats," Lugar said, "but it seems to me that Barack is studying issues that are very important for the country and for the world."

DISAGREEING WITHOUT BEING DISAGREEABLE

Overall, political analysts assessed Obama's record in the Senate as liberal. On most issues Obama voted with the

Obama joins former president Bill Clinton in Reliant Hall, an exposition and conference center in Houston, September 5, 2005. Obama and Clinton, along with former president George H. W. Bush, had traveled to Houston to visit people evacuated from New Orleans after Hurricane Katrina. On returning to Washington, Obama decried the federal government's ineptitude in responding to the Katrina disaster, which he believed was symptomatic of the government's indifference toward the fate of its poorest and most disadvantaged citizens.

majority of Democrats. For example, he supported an increase in the minimum wage and voted to allow federal funding of stem cell research. He voted against a proposed constitutional amendment to make desecration of the American flag a criminal offense. Neither of George Bush's nominees to the Supreme Court, John Roberts and Samuel Alito, received Obama's vote. Obama's first bill, the Higher Education Opportunity Through Pell Grant Expansion Act, was designed to help needy students pay their college tuitions. (The bill never got out of committee because of Republican opposition.) Obama worked with one of the Senate's most liberal members, Russell Feingold of Wisconsin, to win passage of ethics and lobbying reform legislation.

> " I've known Senators, Presidents. I've never known anyone with what seems to me more raw political talent. [Obama] just seems to have the surest way of calmly reaching across what are impenetrable barriers to many people. "
>
> —Laurence Tribe

But Obama also collaborated with Republicans, even conservatives, on a variety of bills. For example, he and Tom Coburn of Oklahoma wrote the Federal Funding Accountability and Transparency Act. The bill, signed into law in September 2006, mandated the creation of an Internet database of federal spending. Increased scrutiny of spending, it was hoped, would cut down on waste and fraud in government contracts and reduce congressionally approved pork-barrel projects.

Barack Obama could point to some moderate legislative successes during his first two years in Washington, but the junior senator from Illinois certainly hadn't gotten any landmark bills passed. That isn't at all surprising: the U.S. Senate puts a premium on seniority, and the influence of new members is generally quite limited.

If it was too early to evaluate the substance of Obama's Senate career, colleagues and congressional observers were quick to compliment his style. In an era of extreme partisanship, Obama sought common ground with Republicans. At a time when shrill, personal attacks were all too common, he insisted on expressing political differences in a civil manner. It was the same approach he had taken as a state senator in Illinois, and before that as president of the *Harvard Law Review*. And it was an approach many Americans welcomed.

"It's such a relief after all the screaming you see on TV," observed Chuck Sweeny, political editor of the *Rockford Register Star*. "Obama is reaching out. He's saying the other side isn't evil. You can't imagine how powerful a message that is. . . ."

GREAT EXPECTATIONS

From the moment Barack Obama arrived in Washington, many people believed that he was destined for greatness. In April 2005, *Time* magazine listed him among the world's 100 most influential people. The British journal *New Statesman*, in an October 2005 article, identified Obama as one of "ten people who could change the world."

Obama had captured the imagination of many Americans with his electrifying keynote address at the Democratic National Convention in 2004. After two years in the Senate, his luster hadn't dimmed. If anything, there was now more excitement surrounding Barack Obama.

In October 2006 Crown published his second book, *The Audacity of Hope: Thoughts on Reclaiming the American Dream*. It quickly became a best seller.

Inevitably, speculation arose about a possible presidential run.

Chapter 10 "WE'VE GOT TO CREATE A BETTER POLITICS"

O n November 7, 2004, less than a week after his election to the U.S. Senate, Barack Obama was asked on the NBC news program *Meet the Press* whether he planned to serve his entire term in the Senate. "Absolutely," Obama answered.

Over the next year and a half, Obama heard variations of the question "Will you run for president?" numerous times. His answer was consistent: he intended to stay in the Senate and would not be a candidate in the next presidential election. Typical was an exchange Obama had with *Meet the Press* host Tim Russert in January 2006. "So you

---

"Barack has become a kind of human Rorschach test," observed Cassandra Butts, senior vice president for domestic policy at the Center for American Progress, a liberal think tank. "People see in him what they want to see." Obama's chances of being elected president hinged largely on whether voters judged his talent, personal appeal, and vision of a better politics more important than lengthy political experience.

will not run for president or vice president in 2008?" Russert asked. "I will not," Obama replied.

By the summer of 2006, however, Obama's answers appeared less categorical. Meanwhile, conjecture in the media went into overdrive. In October *Time* magazine ran a cover story titled "Why Barack Obama Could Be the Next President." That same month Oprah Winfrey declared on her talk show—one of the country's most watched television programs—that she wished Obama would run for president.

Obama and talk show host Oprah Winfrey smile for the cameras at the 36th NAACP Image Awards, held in Los Angeles in March 2005. The awards honor people of color who have made exemplary contributions to the arts or to the cause of social justice. Winfrey would later endorse the presidential bid of her fellow Image Awards winner.

ONCE-IN-A-LIFETIME OPPORTUNITY?

Publicly, Obama—who had been crisscrossing the country to campaign for Democrats—said that his focus was on helping candidates from his party win in the November elections. Only after those elections were over, he declared, would he "think about how I can be most useful to the country and how I can reconcile that with being a good dad and a good husband."

Privately, Obama had begun seeking the advice of prominent Democrats, such as Senator Dick Durbin. "I told him, 'These opportunities come around once, at best twice in a lifetime,'" Durbin recalled. "'You ought to think about that seriously.'"

> ### Obama on Obama
>
> " There's a certain tone in politics that I aspire to that allows me to disagree with people without being disagreeable. "

At campaign events for Democrats and on his book tour to promote *The Audacity of Hope*, Obama was drawing large, enthusiastic crowds. He was, as more than one writer pointed out, like a rock star. His public profile and his popularity might never be higher.

Still, Obama wondered whether his youth and relative lack of experience would undermine a potential run for the White House in 2008. He had, after all, served less than two years in the Senate. Durbin counseled that sticking around the Senate wouldn't make him more attractive as a presidential candidate. In a single term in office, senators cast thousands of votes, and these votes often involve large, complicated bills that include many compromises. Opponents can easily use details from legislation a senator has voted on to paint a distorted picture of the senator's record. That's one of the reasons no sitting senator had been elected president since 1959.

The results of the 2006 elections gave Obama no reason not to consider seriously a presidential run. In the off-year congressional races, Democrats won resoundingly, gaining control of both the Senate and the House of Representatives. Political analysts said the elections were largely a referendum on the Iraq War and, to a lesser extent, on corruption in government. If so, voters strongly rejected the Bush administration's Iraq policy and expressed their displeasure at a lobbying scandal and other ethical lapses, which were committed primarily by Republicans. On both issues, Obama's position appeared solid. He had come out against the war even before the March 2003 invasion of Iraq, and he was a highly visible proponent of ethics reform.

TESTING THE WATERS

After the November congressional elections, Obama began testing the waters for a possible 2008 presidential run. On December 10 he traveled to New Hampshire, site of the first presidential primary election, which was still more than a year away. In past campaigns, candidates who went to New Hampshire that far in advance of the actual voting typically met with small groups in private homes and chatted with citizens outside stores or in diners.

Obama's visit wasn't so low key. In fact, his arrival in New Hampshire was met by an army of reporters and TV crews—some 150 members of the national media in all. Wherever he went, large crowds followed. Aides had booked a small hall for a morning speech but were forced

The junior senator from Illinois fields questions during a press conference before his appearance at a celebration for New Hampshire Democrats in Manchester, December 10, 2006. Obama's enthusiastic reception in the Granite State, site of the first presidential primary election, augured well for a possible run for the White House.

to find a larger ballroom because of the high demand for tickets. Obama spoke to the crowd about hope and optimism, community and common decency. He spoke about ending the war in Iraq and returning the United States to a nation that respects the rule of law and respects other nations. When he was finished, the crowd roared, music blared, and Obama signed autographs and shook hands, smiling all the while.

In the afternoon, Obama addressed a rally for the New Hampshire Democratic Party in Manchester. He ruminated on why he believed he was generating such excitement.

"The reason that I'm getting so much attention right now," he said, "has less to do with me and more to do with you. I think, to some degree, I've become a shorthand or a symbol or a stand-in, for now, of a spirit that the last election . . . represented. And it's a spirit that says, 'We are looking for something different. We want something new.' "

Obama's tumultuous welcome in New Hampshire was in itself something new, veteran political observers noted. "It was," Dan Balz of the *Washington Post* said, "a spectacle. . . . And in talking to people who have been around the track a lot of times in New Hampshire politics, they said they'd never seen anything like it." Of course, whether Barack Obama could continue to generate the same kind of excitement remained to be seen.

MAKING THE DECISION

Obama had made a habit of going back to Hawaii during the Christmas holidays. There he, Michelle, and their daughters would visit with Toot and Maya, and there he would catch up with childhood friends and basketball buddies. This year, however, the trip would be more than just a vacation. Away from the glare of the media and the bustle of Washington, Barack Obama would decide whether or not to run for the presidency of the United States.

There were, of course, political considerations to weigh. His youth, his relative lack of experience in government, and his liberal voting record would provide ammunition for opponents. But, given the so-called slash-and-burn politics of the recent past, it was likely that all manner of personal attacks—true or untrue—would be leveled against Obama. Even the color of his skin could be an unspoken impediment; he had already received threats from bigots.

However, family considerations were paramount in the decision on whether or not to run. A political career inevitably means time away from family, and Michelle always insisted that her husband balance his responsibilities as a lawmaker with his responsibilities as a husband and father. A presidential campaign would create untold demands on Barack's time. Unless Michelle was comfortable with that, he wouldn't run.

> ## Obama on Obama
>
> **"What I am constantly trying to do is balance a hard head with a big heart."**

Aides emphasized that the kind of excitement Obama had been generating often proves fleeting in politics. He might want to wait until his children were older and until he had more political experience before running for president, but by then his opportunity might have passed.

OBAMA ENTERS THE RACE

When the 110th Congress convened in January 2007, Washington was abuzz with rumors that Barack Obama had decided to join the race for president. Obama waited a month before making his official announcement. He chose to declare his candidacy in Springfield, Illinois, outside the Old State Capitol Building. Springfield was where Obama's political career had started. The Old State Capitol was where, nearly a century and a half before, another inexperienced candidate from the Illinois legislature had launched his presidential campaign. That man was Abraham Lincoln.

Saturday, February 10, was a bitterly cold day in Springfield, with a wind chill of 5°F. Nevertheless, an estimated 15,000 people turned out to hear Barack Obama

Outside the Old State Capitol in Springfield, Obama officially announces his candidacy for president, February 10, 2007.

announce that he was running for president. "We all made this journey for a reason," Obama told the crowd.

> It's humbling, but in my heart I know you didn't come here just for me, you came here because you believe in what this country can be. In the face of

war, you believe there can be peace. In the face of despair, you believe there can be hope. In the face of a politics that's shut you out, that's told you to settle, that's divided us for too long, you believe we can be one people, reaching for what's possible, building that more perfect union.

There were two candidates already in the field for the Democratic nomination: Hillary Clinton, the senator from New York and wife of the former president Bill Clinton; and John Edwards, the former North Carolina senator and 2004 Democratic nominee for vice president. Both were better known than Obama, and both had able and experienced people working in their respective campaigns. Winning the nomination would not be easy.

ON THE CAMPAIGN TRAIL

After his Springfield announcement, Obama traveled across the country, sharing his ideas with voters in various states. He discussed specific issues—for example, he advocated a redeployment of American forces in Iraq; called for talks between Iraq and its neighbors, to help quell the sectarian violence in Iraq and end the flow of arms and foreign fighters into the country; and supported a renewed military focus on Afghanistan, where the Taliban was regrouping.

For the most part, however, Obama appealed not so much for different policies as for a different kind of politics. For more than a decade—from the so-called Republican revolution of 1994 to the impeachment of President Bill Clinton in 1998 to the disputed election of George W. Bush in 2000 and the controversial decision to invade Iraq three years later—bitter partisanship had

Early Democratic presidential front-runners Hillary Clinton and John Edwards. Clinton, a senator from New York and the former first lady, and Edwards, the 2004 Democratic vice presidential nominee and former senator from North Carolina, both started the race with greater name recognition than Obama. But both had voted for the 2002 Iraq war authorization, a potentially costly position among an electorate that had turned decisively against the war.

reigned in Washington. Democrats and Republicans seemed constantly at each other's throats, and all too often demonizing political opponents became a substitute for discussing the issues. Obama called for a more civil tone to the national discourse.

The nation, he said at a campaign event in Oklahoma, "can't afford the kind of games we've been playing. . . . It has to do with a politics that is petty, that is small, that is focused on calling folks names and cutting each other up instead of solving the problems of the American people. . . . Politics is not a sport. Politics is not a game. The decisions we make in Washington have consequences for families all across the country. And we've got to create a better politics."

FACING THE NEGATIVE

Obama's appeals for a more high-minded politics had already run into a bit of old-fashioned mudslinging. In January an obscure right-wing magazine reported, and Fox News picked up, a story that Obama had been educated in a madrassa, or Muslim religious school, during his years in Indonesia. The story turned out to be false, but it fueled Internet chatter that Obama secretly harbored radical Muslim sympathies.

Other conservative pundits took Obama to task for his membership in Trinity United Church of Christ. They charged that Trinity's pastor, Jeremiah Wright, was a radical black separatist, and they called on Obama to denounce him.

News reporters and opposition researchers pored over Obama's past for potentially damaging stories. It was discovered that Obama had several unpaid parking tickets in Cambridge, Massachusetts, from the time he was a student at Harvard Law School. He promptly paid them.

The *New York Times* and *Chicago Tribune* reported a more substantive story having to do with Obama's finances and investments. Reporters for those newspapers found that Obama

> ## Obama on Obama
>
> **❝**
>
> **There are some things that I'm absolutely sure about—the Golden Rule, the need to battle cruelty in all its forms, the value of love and charity, humility and grace.**
>
> **❞**

had bought stocks in two companies in which several major donors to his 2004 campaign had a large stake. Both companies had business pending before the federal government. Neither newspaper charged Obama with wrongdoing, but a potential conflict of interest was implied. Obama noted that he hadn't known of the stock purchases—which had been made by the managers of a trust he'd set up—but once he found out in 2005, he immediately sold the stocks, at a loss, to avoid the appearance of impropriety.

ANTIDOTE TO CYNICISM?

These bumps in the road notwithstanding, Obama had much to be optimistic about as the summer of 2007 drew to a close and the primary race began heating up. Presidential preference polls consistently showed him in the top tier of the now-crowded Democratic field, trailing only Hillary Clinton. In addition, through the first two quarters of 2007, Obama had raised more campaign money than any presidential contender in either party, including Clinton. His donor base included more than 250,000 Americans, many of whom had made contributions of $100 or less. This, some political analysts suggested, indicated broad support for Obama's candidacy.

For the junior senator from Illinois, many signs were positive. Yet presidential campaigns are long, grueling, and inherently unpredictable. Throughout American history, a host of promising candidates have stumbled or been tripped up between January's caucuses in Iowa and the general election the following November.

Barack Obama positioned himself as a different kind of candidate—one who would not resort to personal attacks, negative campaigning, or other cynical ploys. Whether that approach was feasible, and whether Obama could live up to the higher standard he'd set for himself in the midst of a heated presidential race, remained to be seen.

Yet even if Obama's candidacy falters, he is likely to be an important figure in American politics for some time to come. When Americans go to the polls to elect the 44th president of the United States, Obama will be just 47—quite young by political standards. He would presumably have other opportunities to seek the nation's highest elective office.

Obama's work in the Senate could also bear important fruit. As a quiet consensus-builder, a self-professed seeker of commonsense solutions to the problems facing the United States, Obama could transcend the shrill partisanship that has poisoned the national discourse in recent years. Perhaps his example might help point the way to a renewed American politics, one in which shared values and common dreams are more significant than individual differences.

That would be a fitting legacy for a man who has spent years searching for the meaning of community.

From the Senate to the Oval Office

In the history of the United States, 15 people who served in the U.S. Senate have gone on to become president. They are: James Monroe, John Quincy Adams, Andrew Jackson, Martin Van Buren, William Henry Harrison, John Tyler, Franklin Pierce, James Buchanan, Andrew Johnson, Benjamin Harrison, Warren G. Harding, Harry S. Truman, John F. Kennedy, Lyndon B. Johnson, and Richard M. Nixon.

However, only two—Harding and Kennedy—went directly from the Senate to the White House.

1961   Barack Hussein Obama is born on August 4 in Hawaii. His father, Barack Obama, is a Kenyan exchange student; his mother, Stanley Ann Dunham, is a native of Kansas.

1963   Father leaves Hawaii to study at Harvard University.

1964   Parents are divorced.

1967   Mother marries Lolo Soetoro, an Indonesian student attending the University of Hawaii. The family moves to Jakarta, Indonesia.

1971   While mother, stepfather, and half sister Maya remain in Indonesia, Obama is sent back to Hawaii to live with his maternal grandparents. Enrolls in the prestigious Punahou School as a fifth grader. His father visits at Christmas.

1973   Mother and half sister return to Hawaii.

1976   Mother and half sister return to Indonesia, leaving Obama to live with his grandparents.

1979   Graduates from Punahou. Enters Occidental College in Los Angeles.

1981   After completing sophomore year at Occidental, transfers to Columbia University in New York.

1982   Father dies in an automobile accident in Kenya.

1983   Graduates from Columbia with a degree in political science.

1985   Accepts a job as a community organizer in Chicago.

1988   Travels to Kenya, where he visits his father's family. Enters Harvard Law School.

1989   Wins position as editor of _Harvard Law Review_. Holds summer internship in Chicago with law firm Sidley & Austin, where he meets Michelle Robinson.

1990   Is elected president of the _Harvard Law Review_, becoming the first black student ever to hold that position.

1991   Graduates magna cum laude from Harvard Law School. Returns to Chicago.

1992   Travels again to Kenya. Marries Michelle Robinson.

1993   Starts work as an associate with law firm of Miner, Barnhill & Galland; begins teaching courses in constitutional law at the University of Chicago Law School.

1995   Memoir, _Dreams from My Father: A Story of Race and Inheritance_, is published. Mother dies of ovarian cancer.

1996   Wins a seat in the Illinois legislature from the 13th Senate District, which is composed largely of Hyde Park on Chicago's South Side.

1999   Daughter Malia is born.

2000   Runs for a seat in the U.S. House of Representatives from Illinois's First District but is soundly defeated in the Democratic primary by popular incumbent Bobby Rush.

2001   Daughter Sasha is born.

2002   In a speech delivered in Chicago in October, declares his opposition to the Bush administration's plans to invade Iraq. Wins reelection to the state senate without opposition.

2003   Announces candidacy for U.S. Senate seat from Illinois.

2004   Wins Democratic primary for U.S. Senate. Delivers keynote address at Democratic National Convention on July 27. In August, *Dreams from My Father* is re-released as a paperback, and it quickly becomes a New York Times best seller. Defeats Republican Alan Keyes in general election for Senate.

2005   Sworn in as U.S. senator.

2006   Second book, *The Audacity of Hope: Thoughts on Reclaiming the American Dream*, is published; it becomes a best seller. Democrats win control of U.S. Senate and House of Representatives.

2007   On February 10 announces candidacy for president of the United States.

Chapter 1: The Speech

p. 9, "Tonight is a particular honor . . ." Barack Obama, Keynote Address at the 2004 Democratic National Convention, July 27, 2004. http://www.barackobama.com/2004/07/27/ keynote_address_at_the_2004_de.php

pp. 9-10, "I stand here . . ." Obama, Keynote Address.

p. 9, "may be the best-written . . ." Joe Klein, "The Democrats' New Face," *Time*, October 16, 2006. http://www.time.com/time/magazine/ article/0,9171,1546302,00.html

p. 10, "If there's a child . . ." Obama, Keynote Address.

pp. 10-11, "there's not a liberal America . . ." Obama, Keynote Address.

Chapter 2: Roots of a Kenyan Kansan

p. 14, "didn't want the Obama blood . . ." Barack Obama, *Dreams from My Father: A Story of Race and Inheritance*, rev. ed. New York: Three Rivers Press, 2004, p. 126.

p. 15, "as educated as any white man." Obama, *Dreams*, p. 414.

p. 18, "I only wanted to teach the chap . . ." Obama, *Dreams*, p. 7.

p. 18, "next to a nigger." Obama, *Dreams*, p. 11.

p. 19, "This fella felt so bad . . ." *Dreams*, p. 11.

p. 19, "Your dad could handle . . ." *Dreams*, p. 8.

p. 20, "one long adventure . . ." *Dreams*, p. 37.

p. 21, "She was interested in religions . . ." Michael Sheridan and Sarah Baxter, "Secrets of Obama Family Unlocked," *Sunday Times* (London), January 27, 2007. http://www.timesonline.co.uk/ tol/news/world/us_and_americas/article1267352.ece

p. 22, "For my mother, . . ." Barack Obama, *The Audacity of Hope: Thoughts on Reclaiming the American Dream*. New York: Crown, 1996, p. 203.

p. 22, "loved drinking." Kim Barker, "History of Schooling

Distorted," *Chicago Tribune*, March 25, 2007.
http://www.chicagotribune.com/news/politics/
chi-0703250340mar25,0,3912421.story

p. 22, "the naughtiest one . . ." Barker, "History of Schooling."

p. 22, "He was built like a bull . . ." Kirsten Scharnberg and Kim Barker, "The Not-So-Simple Story of Barack Obama's Youth," *Chicago Tribune*, March 25, 2007. http://www.chicagotribune.com/news/politics/chi-0703250359mar25,0,7910127.story

pp. 22-23, "He would be very helpful . . ." Scharnberg and Barker, "Not-So-Simple Story."

p. 23, "He didn't say what country . . ." Scharnberg and Barker, "Not-So-Simple Story."

p. 23, "There was always a joke . . ." Jennifer Steinhauer, "A Search for Self in Obama's Hawaii Childhood," *New York Times*, March 17, 2007.

pp. 23-24, "Five days a week . . ." Obama, *Dreams*, pp. 47–48.

p. 25, "the virtues of her . . ." Obama, *Dreams*, p. 49.

p. 25, "Your brains, your character . . ." Obama, *Dreams*, p. 50.

pp. 27-28, "I know that seeing that article . . ." Obama, *Dreams*, pp. 51–52.

p. 28, "For the sake of compression . . ." Obama, *Dreams*, p. xvii.

p. 29, "It might have been an Ebony . . ." Scharnberg and Barker, "Not-So-Simple Story."

p. 29, "what has found its way . . ." Obama, *Dreams*, p. xvi.

p. 30, "necessarily an approximation . . ." Obama, *Dreams*, p. xvii.

Chapter 3: Growing up Black and White in Hawaii

p. 32, "could charm the legs off . . ." Tim Jones, "Obama's Mom: Not Just a Girl from Kansas," *Chicago Tribune*, March 27, 2007.

http://www.chicagotribune.com/news/politics/chi-0703270151mar27,0,3977057,print.story

p. 33,   "Stanley loved that little boy . . ." Scharnberg and Barker, "Not-So-Simple Story."

p. 33,   "I realized that I was to live . . ." Obama, *Dreams*, p. 54.

p. 34,   "Barry was a happy kid . . ." Carlyn Tani, "A Kid Called Barry," *Punahou Bulletin* (Spring 2007). http://www.punahou.edu/page.cfm?p=601

p. 37,   "sort of like the king . . ." Obama, *Dreams*, p. 63.

p. 39,   "He was the kind of guy . . ." Tani, "Kid Called Barry."

p. 39,   "He always had a basketball . . ." Brian Charlton, "Obama Had Multiethnic Existence in Hawaii," Associated Press, February 6, 2007. www.foxnews.com/printer_friendly_wires/2007Feb06/0,4675,ObamaHawaiianRoots,00.html

p. 40,   "He was a leader . . ." Tani, "Kid Called Barry."

p. 40,   "He was just a normal kid . . ." Tani, "Kid Called Barry."

p. 41,   "I was engaged in a fitful . . ." Obama, *Dreams*, p. 76.

p. 42,   "He struggled here with the idea . . ." Steinhauer, "Obama's Hawaii Childhood."

p. 42,   "He never verbalized . . ." Scharnberg and Barker, "Not-So-Simple Story."

pp. 42-43, "It's their world . . ." Obama, *Dreams*, p. 83.

p. 43,   "He was going through . . ." Jackie Calmes, "From Obama's Past: An Old Classmate, a Surprising Call," *Wall Street Journal*, March 23, 2007, p. A1.

pp. 43-44, "It wasn't a race thing . . ." Scharnberg and Barker, "Not-So-Simple Story."

p. 44,   "I don't imagine the decision . . ." Scharnberg and Barker, "Not-So-Simple Story."

 *Chapter Notes*

p. 44,   "his mother was always . . ." Jake Tapper, "Life of Obama's Childhood Friend Takes Drastically Different Path," *Good Morning America*, ABC News, March 30, 2007. http://abcnews.go.com/GMA/story?id=2989722&page=1

p. 45,   "It *is* a big deal . . ." Obama, *Dreams*, p. 88.

p. 45,   "The words were like a fist . . ." Obama, *Dreams*, p. 88.

p. 45,   "They had sacrificed again and again . . ." Obama, *Dreams*, p. 89.

p. 46,   "that black people have . . ." Obama, *Dreams*, p. 91.

p. 47,   "Junkie. Pothead. . . ." Obama, *Dreams*, p. 93.

p. 47,   "We go play hoop." Hans Nichols, "Obama's 'Aloha' Days in the Spotlight," *The Politico*, March 14, 2007, CBS News. http://www.cbsnews.com/stories/2007/03/14/politics/main2567770.shtml

Chapter 4: College Years

p. 48,   "a very thoughtful student . . ." Larry Gordon, "Occidental Recalls 'Barry' Obama," *Los Angeles Times*, January 27, 2007.

p. 48,   "to sum [up] a whole lot . . ." Gordon, "Occidental Recalls."

p. 48,   "I was impressed by the sharpness . . ." Maurice Possley, "Obama's Political Activism Started in College," *Chicago Tribune*, March 27, 2007. http://www.chicagotribune.com/news/nationworld/chi-070329obama-college,1,2683821.story?track=rss/abr

p. 49,   "Clearly the guy had a presence . . ." Gordon, "Occidental Recalls."

pp. 49-50, "I got into politics at Occidental . . ." "Oxy Remembers 'Barry' Obama '83," *Occidental*, January 29, 2007. http://www.oxy.edu/x10722.xml

p. 50,   "Tim seems all right . . ." Obama, *Dreams*, p. 102.

p. 51,   "There's a struggle going on." Obama, *Dreams*, p. 106.

pp. 51-52, "It's happening an ocean away . . ." Obama, *Dreams*, p. 106.

p. 52,   "You wanna know what . . ." Obama, *Dreams*, pp. 108–109.

p. 53,   "You think that's funny? . . ." Obama, *Dreams*, p. 109.

p. 53,   "My identity . . ." Obama, *Dreams*, p. 111.

p. 54,   "If I had to give one adjective . . ." Possley, "Obama's Political Activism."

p. 55,   "only a vague sense . . ." Obama, *Dreams*, p. 128.

Chapter 5: Community Organizer

p. 60,   "very romantic, until . . ." Peter Slevin, "For Clinton and Obama, a Common Ideological Touchstone," *Washington Post*, March 25, 2007, p. A01.

p. 62,   "rub raw the sores . . ." "A Time for Pride," *Time*, May 22, 1964. http://www.time.com/time/magazine/article/0,9171,871153,00.html

p. 63,   "Now, young man . . ." Ryan Lizza, "The Agitator: Barack Obama's Unlikely Political Education," *New Republic*, March 9, 2007. http://www.tnr.com/doc.mhtml?i=20070319&s=lizza031907

p. 63,   "The guy was just totally comfortable . . ." Bob Secter and John McCormick, "Portrait of a Pragmatist," *Chicago Tribune*, March 30, 2007. http://www.chicagotribune.com/news/politics/chi-0703300121mar30,0,7587027.story?page=1

p. 65,   "Whoever can help you . . ." Secter and McCormick, "Portrait."

p. 66,   "Oftentimes . . ." Lizza, "The Agitator."

p. 66,   "a dump—and a place . . ." Obama, *Dreams*, p. 165.

p. 71,   "Unashamedly Black . . ." Trinity United Church of
           Christ website, "Pastor,"
           http://www.tucc.org/pastor.htm

p. 71,   "a congregation with a non-negotiable . . ." Trinity
           United Church of Christ website, "About Us,"
           http://www.tucc.org/about.htm

p. 72,   "there was an explicitly political aspect . . ." Secter
           and McCormick, "Portrait."

p. 72,   "If I joined one of the churches . . ." Secter and
           McCormick, "Portrait."

p. 74,   "He talked about what happens . . ." Secter and
           McCormick, "Portrait."

Chapter 6: Harvard Law

p. 77,   "a faith born out of hardship . . ." Obama, *Dreams*, p.
           429.

p. 78,   "brilliant, charismatic, and focused." Marie C.
           Kodama, "Obama Left Mark on HLS," *Harvard
           Crimson*, January 9, 2007.
           http://www.thecrimson.com/article.aspx?ref=516664

p. 78,   "A lot of people at the time . . ." Michael Levenson
           and Jonathan Saltzman, "At Harvard Law, a Unifying
           Voice," *Boston Globe*, January 28, 2007.
           http://www.boston.com/news/local/
           articles/2007/01/28/at_harvard_law_a_unifying_
           voice/?page=1

p. 79,   "I have worked in the Supreme Court . . ." Jodi
           Kantor, "In Law School, Obama Found Political
           Voice," *New York Times*, January 28, 2007.
           http://www.nytimes.com/2007/01/28/us/politics/28o
           bama.html?pagewanted=1&ei=5070&en=9ca677b7
           86fc2ee9&ex=1179374400

p. 79,   "was populated by a bunch . . ." Kantor, "In Law
           School."

pp. 79-80, "Barack was a stabilizing influence . . ." Levenson and Saltzman, "Unifying Voice."

p. 80, "I worried that it represented the abandonment . . ." Obama, *The Audacity of Hope.*

p. 81, "Whatever his politics . . ." Kantor, "In Law School."

p. 82, "He was in part effective . . ." Kantor, "In Law School."

p. 83, "He then and now . . ." Kantor, "In Law School."

p. 83, "He can enter your space . . ." Kantor, "In Law School."

p. 84, "The years that followed . . ." Kantor, "In Law School."

p. 84, "It was a clarion call . . ." Levenson and Saltzman, "Unifying Voice."

Chapter 7: Putting Down Roots

p. 85, "You can leave your name . . ." Mike Robinson, "Obama Got Start in Civil Rights Practice," Associated Press, February 20, 2007. Boston.com (*Boston Globe* online) http://www.boston.com/news/nation/articles/2007/02/20/obama_got_start_in_civil_rights_practice/

p. 86, "He could have gone . . ." William Finnegan, "The Candidate," *New Yorker*, May 31, 2004. http://www.newyorker.com/archive/2004/05/31/040531fa_fact1?currentPage=1

p. 87, "made a little boy with an absent father . . ." Scharnberg and Barker, "Not-So-Simple Story."

p. 89, "Teaching keeps you sharp . . ." Finnegan, "The Candidate."

p. 90, "a sort of glorified accounting . . ." Obama, *Dreams*, p. 437.

p. 94, "would start a discussion . . ." David Jackson and Ray Long, "Showing His Bare Knuckles," *Chicago Tribune*, April 4, 2007. http://www.chicagotribune.com/news/politics/chi-0704030881apr04,0,6468332.story?page=1

p. 94,   "He did not put it . . ." Jackson and Long, "Bare Knuckles."

pp. 94-95, "I am disappointed . . ." Jackson and Long, "Bare Knuckles."

pp. 95-96, "Why say you're for a new tomorrow . . ." Jackson and Long, "Bare Knuckles."

p. 96,   "there's a legitimate argument . . ." Jackson and Long, "Bare Knuckles."

p. 96,   "To my mind . . ." Jackson and Long, "Bare Knuckles."

Chapter 8: Legislative Lessons

p. 98,   "just give Barack hell." Rick Pearson and Ray Long, "Careful Steps, Looking Ahead," *Chicago Tribune*, May 3, 2007. http://www.chicagotribune.com/news/politics/ chi-0705030101may03,0,1225441.story?page=1

p. 98,   "Barack is viewed in part . . ." Lizza, "The Agitator."

p. 98,   "When it turned out . . ." Pearson and Long, "Careful Steps."

p. 99,   "I knew from the day . . ." Finnegan, "The Candidate."

p. 101,   "You can't always come up with . . ." Finnegan, "The Candidate."

pp. 101-02, "He was passionate in his views . . ." Klein, "Democrats' New Face."

p. 102,   "He's not dogmatic . . ." Pearson and Long, "Careful Steps."

p. 102,   "Obama is an extraordinary man . . ." Finnegan, "The Candidate."

pp. 103-04, "When Congressman Rush and his allies . . ." Edward McClelland, "How Obama Learned to Be a Natural," Salon.com, February 12, 2007. http://www.salon.com/news/feature/2007/02/12/ obama_natural/index.html

p. 104,   "Bobby ain't done nothing wrong." Finnegan, "The

Candidate."

p. 104, "I got a good spanking." McClelland, "How Obama Learned."

p. 105, "I never thought I'd have to . . ." Obama, *The Audacity of Hope*, p. 340.

p. 110, "I don't agree with that . . ." Finnegan, "The Candidate."

p. 110, "I stand before you as someone . . ." BarackObama.com, Remarks of Illinois State Sen. Barack Obama Against Going to War with Iraq, October 2, 2002. http://www.barackobama.com/2002/10/02/ remarks_of_illinois_state_sen.php

pp. 110-11, "Now let me be clear . . ." Remarks of Illinois State Sen. Barack Obama.

Chapter 9: Mr. Obama Goes to Washington

p. 114, "You're a very powerful guy." Pearson and Long, "Careful Steps."

p. 114, "You could help elect . . ." Pearson and Long, "Careful Steps."

P. 114, "Yeah. Me." Pearson and Long, "Careful Steps."

p. 116, "We have shared values . . ." Finnegan, "The Candidate."

pp. 116-17, "People are always asking me . . ." Finnegan, "The Candidate."

p. 118, "He jumped back . . ." Finnegan, "The Candidate."

p. 118, "I am fired up!" "Barack Obama Wins U.S. Senate Democratic Primary in Illinois," *Jet*, April 5, 2004.

p. 121, "a hard-line, academic Marxist." Radio interview, Alan Keyes on the *Steve Malzberg Show* (WABC, New York), August 15, 2004. Alan Keyes Archives, http://www.renewamerica.us/archives/media/

interviews/04_08_15malzberg.htm.

p. 121,   "people of Catholic conscience . . ." Radio interview,
            Alan Keyes on *Kresta in the Afternoon* (Catholic
            radio), September 9, 2004. Alan Keyes Archives,
            http://www.renewamerica.us/archives/
            transcript.php?id=354.

p. 121,   "Christ would not vote . . ." CBS News online,
            "Here's What Jesus Wouldn't Do," September 8,
            2004. http://www.cbsnews.com/
            stories/2004/09/08/politics/main641858.shtml

p. 124,   "I'm feeling very much like the rookie . . ." Jonathan
            Alter, "The Audacity of Hope," *Newsweek*, January 3,
            2005. http://www.msnbc.msn.com/id/6732724/site/
            newsweek/

p. 124,   "I'm so overexposed . . ." Alter, "Audacity."

p. 126,   "At the time, my view . . ." Mike Dorning and
            Christi Parsons, "Carefully Crafting the Obama
            'Brand'," *Chicago Tribune*, June 12, 2007.
            http://www.chicagotribune.com/news/politics/
            chi-obama_senate_recordjun12,0,
            1010006.story?page=1

p. 127,   "He's a sponge . . ." Ben Wallace-Wells, "Destiny's
            Child," *Rolling Stone*, February 7, 2007.
            http://www.rollingstone.com/politics/
            story/13390609/campaign_08_the_radical_roots_of_
            barack_obama

p. 130,   "By investing now . . ." Wallace-Wells, "Destiny's
            Child."

p. 130,   "My comment is not meant . . ." Wallace-Wells,
            "Destiny's Child."

p. 132,   "It's such a relief . . ." Klein, "Democrats' New
            Face."

Chapter 10: "We've Got to Create a Better Politics"

p. 135,   "Absolutely." *Meet the Press* transcript for November
            7, 2004. http://www.msnbc.msn.com/id/6430019/

pp. 135-36, "So you will not run . . ." *Meet the Press* transcript for January 22, 2006. http://www.msnbc.msn.com/id/10909406/

p. 136,   "I will not." *Meet the Press*, January 22, 2006.

p. 137,   "think about how I can be most useful . . ." Klein, "Democrats' New Face."

p. 137,   "I told him, 'These opportunities . . .' " Dorning and Parsons, "Obama 'Brand'."

p. 140,   "The reason that I'm getting . . ." Transcript, PBS Online NewsHour, "Obama's New Hampshire Trip Sparks Interest in 2008 Presidential Race," December 11, 2006. http://www.pbs.org/newshour/bb/politics/ july-dec06/obama_12-11.html

p. 140,   "It was a spectacle . . ." "Obama's New Hampshire Trip."

pp. 142-43, "We all made this journey . . ." BarackObama.com, Full Text of Senator Barack Obama's Announcement for President, Springfield, Illinois, February 10, 2007. http://www.barackobama.com/2007/02/10/ remarks_of_senator_barack_obam_11.php

pp. 144-45, "can't afford the kind of games . . ." Tim Talley, "Obama Draws Enthusiastic Crowd in Okla.," Associated Press, March 19, 2007. ABC News online, http://abcnews.go.com/Politics/ wireStory?id=2965113&CMP=OTC-RSSFeeds0312

Further Reading

Finnegan, William. "The Candidate." *New Yorker*, May 31, 2004.

Lizza, Ryan. "The Agitator." *New Republic*, March 19, 2007.

MacFarquhar, Larissa. "The Conciliator." *New Yorker*, May 7, 2007.

Obama, Barack. *The Audacity of Hope: Thoughts on Reclaiming the American Dream*. New York: Crown Publishers, 2006.

————. *Dreams from My Father: A Story of Race and Inheritance*. New York: Three Rivers Press, 1995. Reprint, 2004.

Sailer, Steve. "Obama's Identity Crisis." *American Conservative*, March 26, 2007.

Wallace-Wells, Ben. "Destiny's Child." *Rolling Stone*, February 7, 2007.

http://obama.senate.gov

> Barack Obama's U.S. Senate website contains press releases, speeches, committee assignments, voting record, and other information.

http://www.barackobama.com

> Obama '08, the official website of Barack Obama's presidential campaign.

http://projects.washingtonpost.com/ congress/members/0000167/

> This page from the U.S. Congress Votes Database, maintained by the *Washington Post*, provides a record of all Barack Obama's Senate votes, as well as his financial disclosure statements and a brief biographical sketch.

Numbers in **bold italics** refer to captions.

Index

Contributors

William Michael Davis earned his degree in Political Science from Villanova University. He is a former Congressional staffer and candidate for the Pennsylvania Legislature. He and his wife, Kathleen, reside in suburban Philadelphia, Pennsylvania.

Photo Credits

Page:

2:	Russell Shively/Shutterstock	81:	© Atlantic Photography–Austin
6:	Paul J. Richards/AFP/	82:	AP Photo/Winslow Townson
	Getty Images	87:	Steve Pope/Landov
8:	AP Photo/M. Spencer Green, File	91:	AP Photo/File
13:	Simon Maina/AFP/	93:	AP Photo/Seth Perlman
	Getty Images	99:	AP Photo/Randy Squires
15:	Bryan Busovicki/Shutterstock	100:	AP Photo/Seth Perlman
16:	© OTTN Publishing;	103:	Scott J. Ferrell/
	(inset) Corbis Images		Contributor/Getty Images
20:	Mosista Pambudi/Shutterstock	105:	Reuters/John Gress/Landov
21:	AP Photo/Tatan Syuflana	106:	PH2 Robert Houlihan,
23:	Chuck Berman/MCT/Landov		USN/Department of Defense
24:	AP Photo/SDN School Menteng 1	109:	Senate TV/Getty Images
26:	Robert W. Kelley/Time Life	115:	Tim Boyle/Getty Images
	Pictures/Getty Images	117:	AP Photo/Jeff Roberson
35:	Photos Courtesy Punahou School	119:	Newhouse News Service/Landov
37:	Chuck Berman/MCT/Landov	120:	AP Photo/Nam Y. Huh
38:	Courtesy Punahou School	123:	Michael Kleinfeld/
40:	Courtesy Punahou School		UPI/Landov
41:	Courtesy Punahou School	125:	U.S. Senate Committee on
43:	AP Photo/Seth Perlman		Veterans' Affairs
46:	(all) Library of Congress	127:	Courtesy Senator Richard G.
49:	Photo by Debbie Martin		Lugar
51:	Cynthia Johnson/Time Life	129:	MC2 Scott Taylor,
	Pictures/Getty Images		USN/Department of Defense
54:	Daniella Zalcman	130:	Richard Carson/Harris County
56:	AP Photo/Nam Y. Huh		Joint Information Center
61:	Milbert O. Brown/MCT/Landov	134:	Jeff Haynes/AFP/Getty Images
62:	AP Images	136:	Arnold Turner/Contributor/
64:	AP Photo		Getty Images
67:	AP Photo/Charles Rex Arbogast	139:	CJ Gunther/epa/Corbis
71:	E. Jason Wambsgans/	142:	Jeff Haynes/AFP/Getty Images
	MCT/Landov	144:	(left) Hillary Clinton for President
74:	Tony Karumba/AFP/		Exploratory Committee; (right)
	Getty Images		John Edwards for President
76:	AP Photo/Karel Prinsloo		

Cover photos: Front Cover: Courtesy Barack Obama

Back Cover: Digital Stock; Russell Shively/Shutterstock